MADE-TO-ORDER

TO ________________,
(FILL IN NAME)

YOU HAVE ALWAYS BEEN:
(PLEASE CHOOSE ONE)

A. THE INSPIRATION FOR MY WORK
B. THE BEST FRIEND IN THE WORLD
C. THE MAN WHOSE PISS I'D MOST LIKE TO DRINK

WITHOUT YOU, I NEVER COULD HAVE BECOME:
(PLEASE CHOOSE ONE)

A. THE GREAT ARTIST I AM
B. SO PROFICIENT AT DRAG
C. THE BITCH EVERYONE'S SCARED OF

BEST ALWAYS –

[signature]

KEY WEST / 2000

The new gay book of lists

The new gay book of lists

LEIGH W. RUTLEDGE

COVER PHOTOGRAPH BY BEL AMI.

MANUFACTURED IN THE UNITED STATES OF AMERICA.
PRINTED ON ACID-FREE PAPER.

THIS TRADE PAPERBACK ORIGINAL IS PUBLISHED BY ALYSON PUBLICATIONS INC.,
P.O. BOX 4371, LOS ANGELES, CALIFORNIA 90078.
DISTRIBUTION IN THE UNITED KINGDOM BY TURNAROUND PUBLISHER SERVICES LTD.,
UNIT 3 OLYMPIA TRADING ESTATE, COBURG ROAD, WOOD GREEN,
LONDON N22 6TZ ENGLAND.

FIRST EDITION: NOVEMBER 1987
SECOND EDITION: JUNE 1996

98 99 00 01 02 a 10 9 8 7 6 5 4 3

ISBN 1-55583-359-4
(PREVIOUSLY PUBLISHED WITH ISBN 1-55583-120-6.)

LIBRARY OF CONGRESS CATALOGING-IN-PUBLICATION DATA
RUTLEDGE, LEIGH W.
THE NEW GAY BOOK OF LISTS / LEIGH W. RUTLEDGE. — 2ND ED.
INCLUDES BIBLIOGRAPHICAL REFERENCES.
ISBN 1-55583-359-4 (ACID-FREE PAPER)
1. GAY MEN—HISTORY—MISCELLANEA. 2. HOMOSEXUALITY—HISTORY—MISCELLANEA. I. TITLE.
HQ76.R895 1996
305.38'0664—DC20 96-19267 CIP

To Richard Donley

Acknowledgments

For their help in providing me with information and assistance, I would like to take a moment to thank the staff of the Academy of Motion Picture Arts and Sciences Library, Sasha Alyson, Peter Borland, Julie Bremer, Robert Clark, David Cooney, Ronda Gettel, Dr. William Halberstadt, Mikey Halliday, Deacon Maccubbin, Scott O'Hara, John Phelps, Felice Picano, John Preston, the staff of the reference department at the Pueblo Memorial Library in Colorado, Edna F. Riley, Phillip B. Roth, R.G. Rowswell, Edward Rutledge, Dr. Elizabeth Rutledge, Chris Schick, Mike Seabrook, Dr. Allan Simmons, Osmo Soljavirta, Sam Staggs, Peter Urbanek, and Edmund White.

A very special thanks to Richard Donley, Paul Hause, and Charlotte Simmons.

However, any errors that may have crept into this work are solely my responsibility.

CONTENTS

Introduction xv

5 memorable gay encounters with dolphins 3

15 provocatively named places 5

19 celebrated gay men better known by a different name 6

Former jobs of 21 gay celebrities 6

32 famous people who have acknowledged having had at least one homosexual experience in their lives 8

12 classic excuses used by "straight" men 9

10 remarkable gay love relationships, how the partners met, and how each relationship ended 10

7 unforgettable gay love offerings 17

15 passionate on-screen mouth-to-mouth kisses between men 19

3 countries in which same-sex marriages are legally recognized 20

2 gay palimony suits 20

7 women who have denied being lesbians 22

14 famous men (and 2 puppets) who have publicly denied being gay 24

3 drag ensembles allegedly worn by former FBI director J. Edgar Hoover 29

10 famous gay men and the length of the FBI's secret surveillance file on each 30

10 U.S. police departments that have actively recruited gay men and lesbians 31

7 famous gay men who served in the U.S. Navy 31

CONTENTS

2 famous gay men who served in the U.S. Air Force 32

17 famous gay or bisexual men who served in the U.S. Army 32

3 famous gay or bisexual men who served in the U.S. Marines 33

14 countries that do not restrict gays from serving in the military 33

7 supposed references to homosexuality in the Bible (King James version) 34

11 admonitions in Leviticus that fundamentalists often conveniently forget about 35

The gospel according to Pat: 12 stupefying quotes from the Rev. Pat Robertson 38

29 famous people who had gay or bisexual sons 41

3 famous men who had gay grandsons 42

Dr. James Packer's 6 signs your son may be turning into a homosexual 42

5 men who were raised as girls 43

8 famous gay men who also had a gay brother 45

10 most common explanations for why people are gay 48

11 memorable suspected causes of homosexuality 49

12 alleged cures for homosexuality 51

Dr. La Forest Potter's 10 characteristics of the average homosexual 55

8 intriguing scientific speculations about gay men 55

7 antiquated medical terms for "homosexuality" 57

16 unusual or archaic expressions for "gay man" 58

5 possible origins for the word "faggot" as a pejorative for "gay man" 61

14 prominent people who have publicly referred to gay men as "faggots" or "fags" 62

7 famous men who disliked the word "gay" 65

22 colorful slang expressions for sodomy 67

16 sex practices and the proper technical terms for each 67

7 popular positions for jacking off and the advantages and disadvantages of each 68

30 picturesque slang expressions for masturbation 70

9 animals, other than humans, that masturbate 70

9 Victorian "cures" for masturbation 72

10 substances often reputed to be aphrodisiacs 75

12 substances reputed to diminish sexual desire and performance 78

12 famous people who believed in the power of aphrodisiacs 78

Ages when 14 famous men first had sex with another man 80

14 men who paid at least once for gay sex 84

13 men who have been paid at least once for their sexual services 85

16 famous men, all reputedly very well-hung 85

Hung like a horse: average erect penis lengths for 10 species 88

6 renowned male nudes 89

3 fascinating severed penises 91

15 famous uncircumcised men 93

15 famous circumcised men 94

15 eighteenth-century slang expressions for "cock" 94

C O N T E N T S

20 nineteenth-century slang expressions for "cock" 95

12 words or phrases that sound obscene but aren't 95

The origins of 7 common sex-related words 96

15 provocatively named businesses 98

Scott O'Hara's top 10 travel destinations for gay sex 99

5 men it would have been better not to go home with 102

23 countries in which homosexual acts between consenting adults have been decriminalized, and when 108

25 countries in which homosexuality is still specifically proscribed by law 109

26 famous men who were arrested on gay sex or morals charges 110

The stories behind 14 of those arrests 111

19 prominent individuals who supported the idea of homosexual rights before 1930 115

46 celebrities who have openly supported gay rights 116

18 celebrity homophobes 117

Ordinary people: 8 gay men who were brutally murdered 122

2 famous men who were victims of gay bashings 128

7 movies that in some way deal with homosexuality, and what the mainstream critics said about each 129

66 notable actors who have appeared in drag in the movies 139

2 unfinished gay novels by famous writers 141

3 suppressed manuscripts of famous gay men 143

The top 10 all-time best-selling gay and lesbian titles at Lambda Rising Bookstore in Washington, D.C. 144

5 "dirty" gay novels written before 1930 145

12 books recently banned, or nearly banned, because of gay and lesbian themes 148

From Sappho to Mapplethorpe: 19 outrageous acts of censorship in the history of gay people 151

26 classic gay graffiti 159

15 terrible historical events that gay people have been blamed for 162

6 early Christians who helped shape the Church's attitude toward homosexuals 162

Heavenly fathers: 6 gay or bisexual popes 165

17 gay-porn stars who died of AIDS complications 167

11 famous people who lied about having AIDS 167

9 gay teachers 171

9 contemporaries of Oscar Wilde and what each said about him 173

4 gay victims of the Nazis 175

7 men who were full- or part-time transvestites 178

14 men who loved boys 184

15 gay or bisexual fathers 188

10 well-known women who married gay or bisexual men 192

10 gay men who didn't let advancing age stop them 195

8 instances of gay lovers buried together 197

Index 200

INTRODUCTION

In the nearly ten years since the original *Gay Book of Lists* was published, the most gratifying thing has been, unexpectedly, the fan mail. I've received hundreds of letters from virtually every part of the United States (though disproportionately from New York City and the South) and from virtually every part of the world (including Poland, South Africa, India, Australia, Fiji, Finland, and the Philippines). The people who have written transcend all age groups—the youngest was thirteen, the oldest in his nineties—all professions, all economic levels.

The letters that mean the most to me are from teenagers.

"Please forgive my penmanship," began one. "I am writing this under the blanket with a flashlight."

"I am fourteen years old," began another, "and am going to the library every day after school to sneak your book off the shelf. The librarian keeps giving me funny looks."

"I am sixteen and want to fall in love with a man so bad, I feel like I'm going to die," wrote another.

"I want to be a drag queen," wrote a fifteen-year-old from Mississippi, "but I'm too young to go buy clothes without raising suspicions. Is it so wrong to be gay and want to dress like a beautiful woman?"

"My mother is making me see a shrink because there aren't supposed to be any homos in our religion," wrote a teenager from Florida. "Please tell me I'm not crazy for wanting a big, muscular, good-looking guy to hold me and protect me and love me."

The examples are almost endless. And, with very few exceptions, every single one of them wrenches something deep in my heart. I answer them all—from the eighteen-year-old in South Dakota who sent me ten dollars in cash and asked if I would please buy him a copy of *Playgirl* and send it to him ("If I tried to buy it here, they would all laugh at me, and my father would kill me") to the sixteen-year-old in Louisiana who asked if I would please come and get him, since his father sprayed weed killer all over him for being "queer" and his mother kept threatening to send him to a priest who performed exorcisms. The most affecting were always the ones that arrived written in pencil on yellow or white legal pads with frantic grammar and iffy spelling. It made one feel—as John Preston and I once discussed (he too was moved by the inordinate number of letters he received from young people)—like opening up a foster home the size of Rhode Island for gay kids.

There were, of course, countless other letters—from attorneys, doctors, fellow writers, members of the armed forces, college professors, even prison inmates. But it was the letters from the young that stuck in my mind and sometimes kept me awake at night. A book can sometimes be a surrogate parent, a surrogate brother, a surrogate mentor. I suppose, back in 1985, I started writing the original *Gay Book of Lists* mostly to give vent to my own frustrations and curiosity. Nearly ten years later, with more than a dozen published books under my belt, I find that I increasingly write with an ever-growing desire to help satisfy the frustration and curiosity of other people.

The idea that the writing of history cannot be both accurate and amusing at the same time is so silly that one is tempted to...well, to laugh. It has always seemed to me that the best cultural chronicles are funny, provocative, and telling in their sometimes trivial details. Even as a youngster I was less interested in the dates and troop movements of the Battle of Waterloo than I was in how Napoleon's agonizing hemorrhoids affected the outcome of the battle (significantly, as it turns out). And when it came to historical figures, from Cleopatra to Lincoln, I was far more fascinated by the minutiae and seemingly trivial details of their lives and loves and hungers than I was in the broader sociological and philosophical implications of their official actions. As the character of Mozart says in *Amadeus*: "Come on, now, be honest—which one of you wouldn't rather listen to his hairdresser than Hercules?" Cliometrics and historiography aside, in the end it often seems to me that the only difference between a historian and a gossip columnist is the size of one's pretensions.

Why, after all this time, have I returned to revise, update, and expand *The Gay Book of Lists*? It is, simply, a labor of love. Writers hold much the same fondness for their first published book as other people hold for their first love. *The Gay Book of Lists* was mine. That it has continued to sell vigorously over the past decade is a source of great pride to me. In returning to it now, I wanted not merely to superficially update the original volume but also to create in many ways a whole new book. To that end, I've dropped numerous lists that seemed dated, while adding more than thirty new ones and revising and updating others. Pop culture moves at something close to the speed of light, and the pace of its daily transformation has without a doubt accelerated over the past ten years with, among other things, the proliferation of cable television. It was with sadness but necessity that I found myself omitting certain names of yesteryear, like Jon-Erik Hexum and Fred Halsted. On the other hand, it was a pleasure to realize that certain other names had rather faded from the limelight, at least for the moment (George Deukmejian and Lyndon LaRouche immediately come to mind).

A few words to the reader before beginning *The New Gay Book of Lists.* First of all, the vast majority of these lists are not meant to be comprehensive. When I write about "5 Memorable Gay Encounters With Dolphins" or "7 Unforgettable Gay Love Offerings" or "5 Men It Would Have Been Better Not to Go Home With," I'm aware that any one of them could be expanded and that, in the case of a list like "18 Celebrity Homophobes," the entries could conceivably go on and on. What I have included largely reflects my own interests and prejudices. Also, although there is some material on lesbians and lesbianism in this book, the overwhelming focus is on gay men.

About dates—especially years of birth—anyone doing research quickly learns that so-called unimpeachable facts from unimpeachable sources may vary widely. I have found, for example, four different years of birth for actor George Maharis—all from reference sources considered completely reliable. In the end, as with other similar conflicts, I finally chose the one that, given other information, seemed most reasonable.

I have been asked through the years why I don't include bibliographies in my books. The answer is simple: so that readers can still afford to buy them. A detailed bibliography for *The New Gay*

Book of Lists would run on to an overwhelming length. For such a seemingly simple and innocuous list as, say, "19 Celebrated Gay Men Better Known By a Different Name," it took nineteen separate sources. Combine that with nearly a hundred different lists, and you have a bibliography that would start to look like a telephone book. And ultimately, how enlightening is it to learn that I found Jeff Stryker's real name in articles in *Out* magazine and *The Advocate*?

As with my other books, I would enjoy hearing from anyone who has comments, additions, corrections, questions, or even complaints about *The New Gay Book of Lists.* Those so inclined should write to:

Leigh W. Rutledge
P.O. Box 1198
Key West, Florida 33041-1198

The new gay book of lists

5 Memorable Gay Encounters With Dolphins

1. Carl Sagan and a dolphin named Peter
In the 1960s astronomer Carl Sagan was visiting a dolphin research center in St. Thomas when he became the object of a young male dolphin's sexual affections. Sagan was in a large indoor pool playing ball with the dolphin, named Peter, when the animal suddenly grazed him. "I felt some protrusion of Peter's lightly brushing my side as he passed," Sagan recalled in his book *The Cosmic Connection.* The dolphin persisted, and it quickly became apparent what the protrusion was and what the dolphin wanted. "I felt," Sagan said later, "like some maiden aunt to whom an improper proposal had just been put." Despite the animal's cheerful single-mindedness, Sagan—though flattered—was, in his words, "not prepared to cooperate."

2. The dolphin of Hawke Bay
In the late 1970s a lone male dolphin set up residence for several months in Hawke Bay, New Zealand. His playfulness and approachability delighted the locals, and after weeks of swimming with the animal—who was given the name Horace—several people achieved a special rapport with him. Among these was diver Quentin Bennett, who often went out in the early morning hours or in the late evening after work to photograph or play with him. During their initial interactions in the water, Bennett noticed that Horace frequently had an erection. At those times Horace's behavior became, according to Bennett, "quite aggressive." However, as they became better acquainted over the next several weeks, the erections ceased, and Horace apparently lost sexual interest in him. "Perhaps he had found out that I am straight," Bennett quipped.

Horace eventually vanished. His fate remains a mystery, though there is speculation he fell victim to an oil spill that occurred in the harbor.

3. The conniving dolphin

In his 1975 book *Dolphins,* Jacques Cousteau relates the anecdote of noted marine biologist Remington Kellogg who was, in Cousteau's words, "passionately loved by a male dolphin in a marineland." According to Cousteau, "the animal tried every means possible to make Kellogg fall into his tank. On two occasions the dolphin succeeded; and on both occasions he manifested his affection in an unmistakable manner."

4. Donald, the pansexual dolphin

One of the most famous wild dolphins to befriend an entire region of a country was Donald, who lived along a several-hundred-mile stretch of Britain over a period of six years during the 1970s. The subject of several books and academic papers as well as a film, *Ride a Wild Dolphin,* Donald regularly played with divers, children, and tourists and offered spectacular rides across the water to the humans he learned to trust. (His passengers held on to his dorsal fin while being whisked over the waves.) On one occasion he even rescued a pet dachshund that had fallen into the sea. His sexual activities became notorious. In the book *Encounters With Whales and Dolphins,* oceanographer Wade Doak describes how Donald liked to rub his "genital areas against male and female swimmers.... [He] would do likewise, even to ejaculation, with mooring ropes, buoys, and the hulls of small dinghies." According to Doak, Donald "was once seen carrying a four-pound bass in his jaws, taking it to the bottom, releasing it, rubbing on it with an erection, taking the fish in his mouth again for a short distance and releasing it." Observers noted, though, that while Donald made sexual advances to adult swimmers, male and female, he never once made similar overtures to children. Donald was last sighted in early 1978.

5. Percy

During the early 1980s another lone male dolphin set up residence along the coast of Britain, this time near Cornwall. The dolphin, who was given the name Percy, regularly chased boats as they came into the harbor, treated onlookers to amazing displays of acrobatics, and enjoyed pursuing windsurfers and knocking them off their boards. With time, Percy developed a trusting relationship with many of the locals, and he soon began sporting an erection and trying to seduce them. One human male swimmer was so enraged that he shoved the dolphin away and gave him a stern lecture. (Percy responded by biting him.) Swedish wildlife writer Lars Lofgren, eager to interact with Percy in the water, quickly found himself being masturbated against. According to Lofgren, Percy "hooked his penis behind my knee and began thrusting.... He persisted like this all day." A few of the townspeople became so upset by stories of Percy's lasciviousness—one local labeled it "buggery"—they threatened to pass ordinances to keep anyone from actually engaging in intercourse with him. However, Percy left the area soon afterward and was never seen again.

15 Provocatively Named Places

1. Gay Head, Massachusetts
2. Dicks Head, Kenya
3. Intercourse, Pennsylvania
4. Dildo, Newfoundland
5. Mount Dick, Adams Island, New Zealand
6. Gays, Illinois
7. Fort Gay, Wyoming
8. Screw River, New Guinea
9. Cumming, Georgia
10. Dykesville, Louisiana
11. Sappho's Leap, Levkás, Greece
12. Dykes Crossroads, Tennessee
13. Oral, South Dakota
14. Big Hole, Montana
15. Blue Ball, Pennsylvania

19 Celebrated Gay Men Better Known by a Different Name

		Better Known as...
1.	Charles Peyton, porn star	Jeff Stryker
2.	RuPaul Andre Charles, entertainer	RuPaul
3.	George Alan O'Dowd, singer	Boy George
4.	Touko Laaksonen, artist	Tom of Finland
5.	Eugene Luther Vidal, author	Gore Vidal
6.	Harris Glenn Milstead, actor	Divine
7.	Wladziu Valentino Liberace, pianist	Liberace
8.	Webb Parmelee Hollenbeck, actor	Clifton Webb
9.	Roy Scherer Jr., actor	Rock Hudson
10.	Nicholas Iacona, porn star	Joey Stefano
11.	Reginald Dwight, singer	Elton John
12.	Roy Halston Frowick, designer	Halston
13.	Arthur Gelien, actor	Tab Hunter
14.	Drew Okin, porn star	Al Parker
15.	Eric Garber, author	Andrew Holleran
16.	Romain de Tirtoff, designer	Erté
17.	Thomas Lanier Williams, playwright	Tennessee Williams
18.	Andrew Warhola, artist	Andy Warhol
19.	John Epperson, entertainer	Lypsinka

Former Jobs of 21 Gay Celebrities

1. Armistead Maupin (b. 1944), U.S. writer
Aide to Republican senator Jesse Helms of North Carolina

2. David Geffen (b. 1943), U.S. media mogul
Busboy at a resort in the Catskills

3. Allen Ginsberg (b. 1926), U.S. poet
Merchant seaman

4. Quentin Crisp (b. 1908), British writer
Male model

5. Michael Feinstein (b. 1956), U.S. entertainer
Piano salesman

6. Boy George (b. 1961), British pop star
Clothing store manager

7. Paul Lynde (1926-1982), U.S. comic actor
Killed and plucked chickens at a meatpacking plant

8. James Coco (1929-1987), U.S. actor
Department store Santa Claus

9. Pedro Almodóvar (b. 1951), Spanish film director
Telephone operator

10. Raymond Burr (1917-1993), Canadian actor
Cabaret singer

11. Ismail Merchant (b. 1936), Indian-born film producer
Messenger for the Indian delegation to the United Nations

12. Tennessee Williams (1912-1983), U.S. playwright
Shoe salesman

13. Harvey Milk (1930-1978), U.S. gay rights activist
Insurance salesman

14. Jack Wrangler (b. 1946), U.S. porn star
Child actor on television

15. Divine (1946-1988), U.S. actor
Hairdresser

16. Malcolm Boyd (b. 1923), U.S. priest and writer
Television producer

17. Edmund White (b. 1940), U.S. writer
Staff writer for the book division of Time Inc.

18. William S. Burroughs (b. 1914), U.S. writer
Pest exterminator, private detective

19. Rock Hudson (1925-1985), U.S. actor
Truck driver

20. Terrence McNally (b. 1939), U.S. playwright
    Private tutor to the son of John Steinbeck
21. J. Edgar Hoover (1895-1972), FBI director
    Librarian

32 Famous People Who Have Acknowledged Having Had at Least One Homosexual Experience in Their Lives

1. Voltaire (1694-1778), French philosopher
2. Giovanni Giacomo Casanova (1725-1798), Italian adventurer and libertine
3. Leo Tolstoy (1828-1910), Russian author
4. Winston Churchill (1874-1965), British statesman
5. Carl Jung (1875-1961), Swiss founder of analytical psychology
6. Whittaker Chambers (1901-1961), U.S. journalist
7. Tallulah Bankhead (1903-1968), U.S. actress
8. Alan Paton (1903-1988), South African writer
9. Louise Brooks (b. 1906), U.S. silent screen star
10. Harold Robbins (b. 1916), U.S. writer
11. Arthur C. Clarke (b. 1917), British science-fiction writer
12. Carson McCullers (1917-1967), U.S. writer
13. Marlon Brando (b. 1924), U.S. actor
14. Marcello Mastroianni (b. 1924), Italian actor
15. Richard Burton (1925-1984), British actor
16. Tiny Tim (b. 1925), U.S. performer
17. Hugh Hefner (b. 1926), U.S. publisher of *Playboy* magazine
18. James Dean (1931-1955), U.S. actor
19. Al Goldstein (b. 1936), U.S. publisher of *Screw* magazine
20. Judy Carne (b. 1939), British comedian
21. Joan Baez (b. 1941), U.S. folksinger and political activist

22. Janis Joplin (1943-1970), U.S. rock singer
23. Billie Jean King (b. 1943), U.S. tennis pro
24. Pete Townshend (b. 1945), British musician
25. Oliver Stone (b. 1946), U.S. film director
26. David Bowie (b. 1947), British rock singer
27. Daryl Hall (b. 1948), U.S. pop singer
28. Grace Jones (b. 1952), Jamaican-born singer and actress
29. Eric Bogosian (b. 1953), U.S. actor
30. Howard Stern (b. 1954), U.S. media personality
31. Madonna (b. 1958), U.S. pop singer
32. Scott Valentine (b. 1958), U.S. actor

12 Classic Excuses Used by "Straight" Men

1. "Man, was I drunk last night. I don't remember a thing."
2. "I needed the money, and he offered me fifty bucks."
3. "I was thinking of a girl the whole time."
4. "Boy, was I beat last night. I was out like a light the moment my head hit the pillow."
5. "It doesn't make you queer so long as you don't kiss."
6. "It doesn't make you queer so long as you don't suck cock."
7. "It doesn't make you queer so long as you don't get fucked in the ass."
8. "There were no women in jail [the Persian Gulf, Vietnam, the job site in Alaska, etc.]."
9. "My analyst said I should try it."
10. "My wife is pregnant."
11. "I was just curious."
12. "I was just hanging out at the bar doing research for my college term paper."

NOTE: One of the most memorable examples of Excuse #4—"I was asleep through the whole thing"—occurred in 1994, when a U.S.

Army sergeant in California was court-martialed for sexually assaulting another serviceman in his sleep. The sergeant, Paul Whitner, was accused of entering the room of Specialist Richard Hill in the middle of the night and undressing him, caressing him, biting him, calling him "beautiful," and then fellating him to the point of orgasm. In his statement to investigators, Hill claimed he was sound asleep through the entire "assault." The Army believed him and granted him immunity from prosecution while pursuing charges against Whitner.

10 Remarkable Gay Love Relationships, How the Partners Met, and How Each Relationship Ended

1. William Haines and Jimmy Shields

How long they lasted: 47 years

How they met: Haines was the popular, handsome star of numerous MGM comedies in the 1920s and '30s. Shields was his equally handsome stand-in on the MGM lot. The two became lovers when they were both in their mid twenties.

The relationship at a glance: Haines and Shields were inseparable, recognized by many as just another Hollywood couple—so well recognized that Louis B. Mayer, then head of MGM, finally called Haines into his office and delivered an ultimatum: "I'm going to give you a choice. You're either to give up that boyfriend of yours, or I'll cancel your contract." Haines chose Jimmy. The two eventually opened a successful interior decorating service that catered to such famous clients as Joan Crawford, Carole Lombard, George Cukor, and Walter Annenberg. Unfortunately, in 1936, they made national headlines for an entirely different reason when they were brutally beaten by outraged representatives of the notorious White Legion, California's answer to the Ku Klux Klan, which assaulted them and several of their gay friends as they were leaving a gay party in conservative Orange County.

How it ended: Haines and Shields weathered the attack and its attendant publicity, and the relationship ended only with Haines's death from cancer in 1973. Shields committed suicide the following year. His suicide note read: "It's no good without Billy."

2. Samuel Barber and Gian Carlo Menotti

How long they lasted: 44 years

How they met: The two men met and fell in love while they were students at the Curtis Institute of Music in Philadelphia. Menotti was seventeen, Barber was eighteen.

The relationship at a glance: After they met, they traveled to Italy together with the prize money Barber had recently won for his "Violin Sonata." The trip was spent, according to one biographer, "basking in the beauty of the countryside and taking part in the gossip of Menotti's Italian relatives." For more than four decades after that, the two men enjoyed a vibrantly creative relationship, much of which was spent at their renowned estate, Capricorn, at Mount Kisco, New York. Barber became most famous for his "Adagio for Strings" (composed when he was in his early twenties), Menotti for his operas *Amahl and the Night Visitors* and *The Medium.* The two sometimes collaborated on their work: For example, in 1958 Menotti wrote the libretto for Barber's Pulitzer prize-winning opera *Vanessa.*

How it ended: The relationship came apart after Menotti, then in his sixties, fell in love with a younger man. Capricorn was sold, and the two men went their separate ways. Barber died in 1981.

3. Peter Pears and Benjamin Britten

How long they lasted: 40 years

How they met: Pears and Britten first met, briefly, in 1934, in a broadcast studio of the BBC, where Pears was singing in a radio program. Britten was twenty-one and had just finished college, Pears was twenty-four and a member of the BBC Singers. However, despite occasionally socializing together, they didn't become lovers until two years later. It was the death of a close mutual friend in a plane crash that finally brought them together: Pears had the unenviable task of sorting through the friend's papers, and Britten (who had just lost his mother) offered his help and moral support.

The relationship at a glance: Britten composed most of his solo vocal works and all of his major tenor roles specifically for Pears. The operas included *Peter Grimes, A Midsummer Night's Dream, Billy Budd,* and *Death in Venice*—the most important English operas since Purcell. "Honestly, you are the greatest artist that ever was," Britten wrote Pears shortly before the Metropolitan Opera premiere of *Death in Venice* in 1974. "What have I done to deserve such an artist and man to write for?"

How it ended: Their extraordinarily intimate and adoring relationship ended with Britten's death in 1976. Britten died in Pears's arms. "I must die first, before you," Britten had always told him, "because I don't know what I would do without you."

4. Christopher Isherwood and Don Bachardy

How long they lasted: 33 years

How they met: Isherwood and Bachardy were introduced to one another at a party in Santa Monica, Calif., in 1953. Isherwood was a handsome, successful 48-year-old writer; Bachardy was an unusually boyish eighteen-year-old with a love of sketching and a slight though charming gap in his front teeth. Bachardy later recalled, "We all drank a lot—which I almost never did in those days—and at the end of it Chris and I kissed and hugged each other and lost our balance and fell right through a window."

The relationship at a glance: The relationship initially scandalized many of Isherwood's friends because of the age difference, yet it lasted more than thirty years. During that time Isherwood dedicated several of his books—including *Christopher and His Kind* and *Down There on a Visit*—to Bachardy. Bachardy, having become a successful artist in his own right, often provided affectionate drawings of Isherwood for the books' covers. "When you fall in love," Isherwood once explained, "you feel you've discovered the bird of paradise, the magic person from the Other Land. You suddenly see a human being in all his magic extraordinariness. And you know that you can never understand him, never take him for granted. He's eternally unpredictable—and so you are to him, if he loves you. And that's the tension. That's what you hope will never end."

How it ended: The relationship ended with Isherwood's death, at the age of 82, in 1986.

5. Edward Carpenter and George Merrill

How long they lasted: 30 years

How they met: They met by chance in a railway carriage one day in 1898. Carpenter was fifty-four and renowned as a progressive writer, amateur naturalist, and social crusader; he was called "the British Thoreau." Merrill was twenty-six and a working-class boy from the slums of Sheffield. They became lovers and began living together shortly after they met.

The relationship at a glance: One afternoon a missionary called at their country home at Millthorpe to try to convert the two men to Christianity. "Don't you want to go to heaven?" the missionary demanded. Merrill replied, "Listen, we're in heaven right here." The Millthorpe house became famous as a haven for activists and visionaries—both gay and straight—from all over the world. (It was after a visit there, and after Merrill casually touched him on the buttocks, that E.M. Forster was inspired to write *Maurice*.)

How it ended: The relationship ended with Merrill's death in 1928. Carpenter died the following year.

6. Kenneth Halliwell and Joe Orton

How long they lasted: 16 years

How they met: Halliwell and Orton met in 1951 as students of the Royal Academy of Dramatic Art in London. Halliwell was twenty-five, flamboyant, and had intense aspirations of becoming a great actor or writer. Orton was seventeen and ambitious but unpolished; before RADA, he'd attended a vocational school with the expectation of becoming a typist or secretary.

The relationship at a glance: The relationship evolved into a gay nightmare version of *Pygmalion*. Halliwell, the mentor, tutored Orton in writing and classical literature. Orton was the eager student. Together they wrote a handful of novels and short stories, which were consistently rejected by publishers. After the two of them spent six months in jail in 1962 for defacing over seventy library books (among other things, they wrote obscene versions of jacket copy and then pasted them into the books), Orton began writing on his own. Within five years, as the author of such celebrated plays as *Entertaining Mr. Sloane, Loot,* and *What the Butler Saw,* he was an international success and the toast of London.

How it ended: JOE ORTON IS A SPINELESS TWAT! Halliwell wrote on the wall of their one-room apartment in May 1967. He felt increasingly left by the wayside in Orton's life. Orton's friends didn't help matters: One of them condemned Halliwell as "a middle-aged nonentity" to his face. Finally, on August 9, 1967, Halliwell, in a rage, bludgeoned Orton to death with a hammer. After delivering nine crushing blows to Orton's skull, he committed suicide with almost two dozen Nembutals.

7. Tennessee Williams and Frankie Merlo

How long they lasted: 15 years

How they met: Williams and Merlo met in Provincetown in the summer of 1947, slept together for one night, and then parted ways. Williams was thirty-six and had just finished his most recent play, *A Streetcar Named Desire*; Merlo—handsome, muscular, and emotionally generous—was a 25-year-old veteran of the U.S. Navy. They met again in New York City the following year. By autumn Merlo had moved in with the playwright.

The relationship at a glance: "Everyone who ever met Frank Merlo found him a marvelous man," Christopher Isherwood once commented. "He was just plain good." "Merlo was a wonderful man for Tennessee," another friend remarked. "Number one for his devotion to Tennessee, a real devotion.... Tennessee was being really loved and taken care of by Frank, and he needed that a great deal." The later years of their relationship found Williams and Merlo increasingly at odds (often over the issue of sexual fidelity), and they sometimes separated for long periods of time.

How it ended: The relationship endured until Merlo's death from lung cancer in 1963. "When he died," Williams later recalled, "I went to pieces. I retreated into a shell. For nine months I wouldn't speak to a living soul. I just clammed up. I wouldn't answer the telephone, and I wouldn't leave the house." Even after recovering from his initial grief, Williams descended into what he described as "a seven-year depression" over Merlo's death.

8. Edward II and Piers Gaveston

How long they lasted: 14 years

How they met: Gaveston was the muscular and athletic sixteen-year-old orphaned son of a Gascon knight. Edward was fourteen, the son of King Edward I, and a disappointment to his family since he had little interest in politics or war. Gaveston was initially brought over from France in 1298 to be a tutor and companion to the young Edward.

The relationship at a glance: The two boys soon embarked on a passionate relationship that enraged the royal court, especially when Edward, after ascending the throne in 1307 at the age of twenty-three, began giving Gaveston land, money, and substantial political power. Under intense political pressure from his advisers, Edward banished Gaveston at least twice—once in 1309 and again in 1311—but on both occasions Edward had a change of heart and brought him back. Renowned for his superb athletic skills—and for his arrogance—Gaveston was adored by Edward but loathed by almost everyone else.

How it ended: The fourteen-year relationship came to a violent end when Gaveston was finally abducted, imprisoned, and beheaded by a conspiracy of outraged barons. Fifteen years later Edward was himself murdered—by the insertion of a red-hot iron into his anus—on orders from his wife, Isabella, and her ambitious lover, Mortimer.

9. Walt Whitman and Peter Doyle

How long they lasted: 8 years

How they met: Doyle and Whitman met in Washington, D.C., sometime in the fall or winter of 1865. Whitman was forty-six. Doyle, a former Confederate soldier, was an eighteen-year-old streetcar conductor. The two met during a violent rainstorm when Whitman jumped aboard Doyle's streetcar to escape the downpour.

"He was the only passenger," Doyle later wrote, "it was a lonely night, so I thought I would go and talk with him... We were familiar at once—I put my hand on his knee—we understood. He did not get out at the end of the trip—in fact went all the way back with me."

The relationship at a glance: After their initial meeting, Whitman frequently accompanied Doyle on his trolley route. In fact, the two of them together became a regular sight around Washington. Whitman attempted to tutor him in math, astronomy, and literature. However, Doyle never fully understood or appreciated Whitman's poetry; on the contrary, he lost the original manuscript of Whitman's "Drum-Taps," which Whitman had given him as a present, and he regarded "Leaves of Grass" as "a great mass of crazy talk." Despite its joys, the relationship caused Whitman some confusion and guilt, and he vowed to himself, on at least one occasion, never to see Doyle again. Nonetheless, Whitman wrote him, "I don't know what I should do if I hadn't you to think of and look forward to."

How it ended: Although the two men didn't live together, their intimacy lasted for approximately eight years, until Doyle was supplanted in Whitman's affections by an eighteen-year-old errand boy the poet met at a printing shop.

10. Paul Verlaine and Arthur Rimbaud

How long they lasted: 2 years

How they met: At the time of their meeting, Verlaine was twenty-seven, married, and one of the most influential French poets of his generation. Rimbaud was only seventeen. They met in Paris in 1871, after a correspondence in which Rimbaud had sent the older man some of his poems. Rimbaud—who was just starting to receive recognition for his astonishingly original verse—was, by all accounts, shockingly beautiful. He was also largely broke.

The relationship at a glance: Initially Verlaine and his wife, Mathilde, took Rimbaud under their wing. Shortly afterward, however, Verlaine fell desperately in love with the younger man, deserted his wife (and their infant son), and fled Paris with Rimbaud at his side to travel throughout Europe. It was a turbulent two years, marked by heavy drinking, quarreling, emotional sado-masochism, and jealousy. "I am having a bad dream," Verlaine wrote his wife. "I'll come back someday." It was also one of the most creative periods in Verlaine's life. He wrote, among other things, his "Romances Without Words" while carousing through France and Belgium with Rimbaud.

How it ended: The affair ended when Verlaine, apparently attempting suicide, instead turned his gun on Rimbaud. Rimbaud, who suffered a gunshot wound to the wrist, summoned the police. Verlaine was arrested and served an eighteen-month prison sentence for attempted manslaughter. After his release, Rimbaud would have nothing further to do with him.

7 Unforgettable Gay Love Offerings

1. Independence for Arabia

British soldier and adventurer T.E. Lawrence dedicated his masterpiece, *The Seven Pillars of Wisdom,* "To S.A."—Salim Ahmed, a handsome Arab boy he had loved. Lawrence also claimed that the motivation during his entire campaign to drive the Turks from Arabia had been "personal." "I liked a particular Arab," he said, referring to Ahmed, "and I thought that freedom for the race would be an acceptable present."

2. *Pictures at an Exhibition*

Mussorgsky's famous work, one of the most popular pieces in the classical repertoire, was based on an exhibit of watercolors by the handsome young architect and painter Viktor Gartman, with whom Mussorgsky was painfully in love. Gartman's death in 1874, at the age of thirty-nine, devastated Mussorgsky, who wrote much of *Pictures* in a grief-stricken, drunken stupor. "Why should a dog, a horse, a rat live on," Mussorgsky wrote a friend, "and creatures like Gartman must die!" The completed *Pictures,* later orchestrated by Ravel, was dedicated to Gartman's memory.

3. The *Pathétique* symphony

Tchaikovsky's Sixth Symphony, the *Pathétique,* was dedicated to his nephew, Vladimir Davidov, with whom the composer was deeply in love. Tchaikovsky wrote of the symphony, "I love it as I have never loved a single one of my offspring."

4. *The Counterfeiters*

In 1916 André Gide began work on his only novel, *The Counterfeiters,* in order to woo and impress sixteen-year-old Marc Allegret, with whom Gide, then forty-seven, had fallen in love. Allegret was apparently suitably charmed: The two enjoyed a long, intimate relationship. Allegret later became a well-known film director.

5. Royal patronage

After falling in love with composer Richard Wagner, King Ludwig II, the eighteen-year-old monarch of Bavaria, paid off Wagner's enormous debts, provided him with housing and an income, and arranged for extravagant productions of Wagner's operas in Munich—all in an attempt to keep the composer near him. Even after the two broke off their intimacy, Ludwig continued to provide Wagner with homes, financial support, and the critical funds needed to finish the opera house at Bayreuth, which Wagner was building in the 1870s.

6. An inscription

When archaeologists excavated the ruins of Pompeii and Herculaneum, they discovered a profusion of ancient graffiti, much of it erotic, scribbled on various walls throughout the cities. One such inscription records the relationship enjoyed by two men and reads simply: "Auctus fucked Quintius here." We know nothing about either Auctus or Quintius, except for the pleasure they shared two thousand years ago.

7. The most spectacular funeral in history
Alexander the Great had the body of his dead lover, Hephaestion, burned atop an awesome 200-foot pyre, erected at a cost of over 10,000 talents, equivalent to roughly $60 million today. The pyre, which took months to complete, contained tiers of sculpted ships, centaurs, bulls, sirens, lions, and wreaths, all in combustible softwood. Plans were made for an even more spectacular lasting memorial: the carving of Mount Athos, the entire mountain, into a huge likeness of Hephaestion, so large that a town of 10,000 people could fit in the palm of the statue's left hand. However, work on the project was never begun, and Alexander himself died less than a year after Hephaestion's passing.

15 Passionate On-Screen Mouth-to-Mouth Kisses Between Men

1. Rod Steiger and John Phillip Law: *The Sergeant* (1968)
2. Michael York and Anthony Corlan: *Something for Everyone* (1970)
3. Peter Finch and Murray Head: *Sunday Bloody Sunday* (1971)
4. Gerard Depardieu and Robert De Niro: *1900* (1977)
5. Alan Bates and George de la Pena: *Nijinsky* (1980)
6. Michael Ontkean and Harry Hamlin: *Making Love* (1982)
7. Christopher Reeve and Michael Caine: *Deathtrap* (1982)
8. Daniel Day-Lewis and Gordon Warnecke: *My Beautiful Laundrette* (1986)
9. Hugh Grant and James Wilby: *Maurice* (1987)
10. James Wilby and Rupert Graves: *Maurice* (1987)
11. Stevan Rimkus and Gary Oldman: *Prick Up Your Ears* (1987)
12. Gary Oldman and Alfred Molina: *Prick Up Your Ears* (1987)
13. Matthew Broderick and Brian Kerwin: *Torch Song Trilogy* (1988)
14. Russell Crowe and John Poulson: *The Sum of Us* (1994)
15. Linus Roache and Robert Carlyle: *Priest* (1995)

3 Countries in Which Same-Sex Marriages Are Legally Recognized

1. Denmark
2. Norway
3. Sweden

2 Gay Palimony Suits

1. *Brent Plott* v. *Merv Griffin*
In 1991 Griffin's former bodyguard and horse trainer, Brent Plott, filed a $250-million palimony suit against him, claiming that he and Griffin had been lovers for four years and that Griffin had promised to support him for life. "I gave him sex, companionship, emotional support, business advice, and anything else he wanted," Plott told the press. "But I ended up with nothing. He used me." Plott, who referred to himself in one interview as Griffin's "sexual plaything," also claimed to have made critical production decisions in the development of Griffin's wildly successful syndicated game show *Wheel of Fortune,* including choosing Vanna White as the program's letter-turning hostess. "These allegations are garbage!" Griffin responded. "There is absolutely no truth to Mr. Plott's claims." Griffin, who was often seen in public on the arm of purported longtime "fiancée" Eva Gabor, also denied widespread rumors he is gay. "This is a shameless attempt to extort money from me," he claimed. However, a former employee of the Helmsley Palace—where Griffin often stayed in New York—revealed to one newspaper that he had frequently secured male prostitutes for Griffin's entertainment, and one of Griffin's California neighbors told a reporter from *People* magazine, "There's always an entourage

of muscle-boy, weight-lifting types with him." Regardless of the public debate over Griffin's sexuality, a judge later dismissed Plott's lawsuit for lack of evidence.

2. ***Scott Thorson* v. *Liberace***

When Scott Thorson and Liberace met in 1974, Thorson was a troubled, good-looking seventeen-year-old who had spent much of his life in and out of foster homes. They met when Thorson attended one of Liberace's Las Vegas shows and was invited backstage to meet the flamboyant entertainer. Two weeks later Thorson moved into Liberace's home. For the next six years Thorson acted as chauffeur and bodyguard and even on occasion escorted Liberace onstage when he performed. Behind the scenes the two had sex, frequently went shopping together (sometimes they would "wake up in the middle of the day and go out and buy homes on a whim," Thorson said later), and enjoyed what was often a prosaic domestic existence together, watching movies and playing with Liberace's numerous pampered dogs. Eight years after they met and shortly after he was allegedly evicted from Liberace's home by force, Thorson went public with the affair and sued the pianist for $113 million in palimony. "We lived together as man and wife," he told the press. In the suit Thorson alleged that he had not only given up a promising career as a dancer in order to tend to Liberace's needs but had also undergone plastic surgery, to Liberace's specifications, in order to be more physically appealing to the entertainer. Liberace denied the claim and issued a statement asserting that the suit was "an outrageous, ambitious attempt to assassinate my character." Eventually, however, he reached an out-of-court settlement with Thorson, which included $95,000 in cash, a 1960 Rolls-Royce, and two dogs. The two men were reconciled, by telephone, just prior to Liberace's death from AIDS complications in 1987. "I told him I was very sorry about everything," Thorson said, "and I said, 'I love you.' "

7 Women Who Have Denied Being Lesbians

1. Imelda Marcos (b. 1931), widow of Philippine dictator Ferdinand Marcos

In 1984 she told a Manila newspaper that, contrary to widespread rumors, she is not a lesbian. "You know, when Cristina Ford used to come here, everybody would say I was a lesbian," she said. "One time we were with Placido Domingo, the singer, and there were about twelve women at one round table, and all of them did not want to touch me with a ten-foot pole because I was such a queen of the lesbians!" Although she has denied being a lesbian herself, Mrs. Marcos has often expressed warm feelings of camaraderie with both lesbians and gay men and has frequently claimed that Philippine homosexuals were among her husband's most ardent supporters.

2. Dolly Parton (b. 1946), U.S. entertainer

In her autobiography, *Dolly: My Life and Other Unfinished Business,* Parton denied gossip she is a lesbian and is lovers with her close friend and personal assistant Judy Ogle. "I could titillate you by telling you that Judy and I make love," Parton wrote, "but then I'd have to disappoint you with the truth.... We're just good and pure, sweet, fun-loving friends." Rumors about Parton's sexuality have been fueled, in part, by the near-total public invisibility of her husband, Carl Dean.

3. Julie Andrews (b. 1935), British-U.S. entertainer

Andrews has not only publicly denied she is a lesbian but has also dismissed stories that her husband, film director Blake Edwards (*The Pink Panther, Victor/Victoria*), is a homosexual and that the two of them enjoy a marriage of convenience. "The gutter press usually prints something silly," she has said, "and it gets picked up at the hairdresser's by a whole bunch of ladies or gentlemen, and before you know it, the gossip becomes fact." She has also denied rumors that she and Carol Burnett were once lovers and that she, her husband, and Rock Hudson enjoyed an ongoing ménage à trois (and frequented leather bars together) during the filming of *Darling Lili* in the late '60s. "My recollection is, we all giggled about [the stories]," she told an interviewer. She has, however, acknowledged that, like many women, she has sometimes wondered what it would be like to have an affair with another woman.

4. Whitney Houston (b. 1963), U.S. singer
In response to long-standing speculation about her sexuality, Houston exploded at a reporter from *Rolling Stone* who asked her outright if she were a lesbian. "That's bullshit," she exclaimed. "I have denied it over and over again, and nobody's accepted it." She blamed the stories on her soaring popularity, which she said made her an easy target for gossipmongers to "fuck with." The rumors persisted after her 1992 marriage to singer Bobby Brown. "You know how nasty it is that I'm a married woman and they're still calling me gay?" she told an interviewer. "If I was gay, I swear I would say it. But I ain't ever liked a woman in my bed. I swear to God. I'm so fucking tired of that question. And I'm tired of answering it." Rumors about her sexuality had centered for years on her inseparable friendship with childhood pal and close adviser Robyn Crawford.

5. Madonna (b. 1958), U.S. entertainer
After tantalizing the public for months with what appeared to be an ongoing lesbian romance with comedian Sandra Bernhard (among other things, the two made a joint appearance on *Late Night With David Letterman* and strongly implied they were sleeping together), Madonna finally told *Vanity Fair* in 1990 that she is not a lesbian and that Bernhard was not her lover. The entertainer reiterated her denial in a 1994 British magazine interview. "I have good friends who are lesbians," she explained, "and the public assumes I'm sleeping with them.... I'm not a lesbian. I love men."

6. Kirstie Alley (b. 1955), U.S. actress
A 1990 *Village Voice* column alleged that Alley was "a daughter of Sappho" and implied that her husband, Parker Stevenson, was a closet homosexual. "It's funny in a pathetic way," Alley said, denying the rumor. "It must be a last resort to find something controversial about us." Her publicist told the press, "It's just too stupid to comment on."

7. Kathleen Sullivan (b. 1954), U.S. anchorwoman and TV personality
In 1994 Sullivan denied reports that she and Martina Navratilova had once been lovers. "She's a very good friend," Sullivan told *People* magazine, "and at times she stayed in my apartment when she was in New York, but we couldn't be more far apart with our sexual preferences."

14 Famous Men (and 2 Puppets) Who Have Publicly Denied Being Gay

1. Tom Cruise (b. 1962), U.S. actor
Dogged by rumors of homosexuality since a supermarket tabloid coyly alluded to the possibility in the late '80s, Cruise told *Vanity Fair* in 1994, "Look at all the stuff that I've heard about myself. That I'm a misogynist. I'm a homosexual. I'm brainless. How can I be all of these things?" Cruise, a Scientologist, added that he didn't regard the rumors as an "indictment." "I don't care if people are Martians," he emphasized. "I really don't care. Straight. Gay. Bisexual. Catholic. Jewish." Asked about all the speculation over her husband's sexuality, Cruise's wife, actress Nicole Kidman, told an interviewer, "I'll bet all my money…that he doesn't have a gay lover, that he doesn't have a gay life."

2. Pope Paul VI (1897-1978)
When the Italian magazine *Tempo* published an article in 1976 asserting that he was a practicing homosexual, Pope Paul VI took the unprecedented step of issuing a denial in a public speech from his balcony overlooking St. Peter's Square. He called the magazine's assertions "a horrible and slanderous insinuation" and implored Catholics everywhere to "pray for our humble person, who has been made the target of scorn…by a certain press lacking dutiful regard for honesty and truth." Shortly after his denial, Italian police began mass confiscations of the magazine on the grounds that it had libeled the Catholic Church.

3. Magic Johnson (b. 1959), U.S. basketball player
After a 1991 press conference at which Johnson acknowledged his HIV-positive status, rumors began to circulate that he had acquired the virus through homosexual activities. The basketball star not only denied he is gay but also claimed to have never had a homosexual experience in his life. "If I were gay, it would have come out," he remarked. "That's just something that you're not going to be able to hide from the media." At the same time, he chided fans who expressed relief to learn he wasn't gay; he denounced such distinctions over acquisition of the virus as "stupid." Johnson has conceded having had sex with over a thousand women during his lifetime.

4. Prince Edward (b. 1964), youngest son of Queen Elizabeth II
After the British tabloid press tried to romantically link him with a British actor, the young royal, long rumored to be gay, finally denied he is homosexual. "It's just outrageous to suggest this sort of thing," he complained. "It's so unfair to me and my family. How would you feel if someone said you were gay?"

5. Keanu Reeves (b. 1964), U.S. actor
Reeves flatly denied being gay in a profile in *Interview* magazine. "But," he quickly added with a smile, "ya never know." "Well, I mean, there's nothing wrong with being gay," he said later, "so to deny it is to make a judgment. And why make a big deal of it?… It's just gossip, isn't it?" In regard to rumors that he and openly gay

entertainment mogul David Geffen were once secretly married, Reeves said, "I've never met the man."

6. Michael Jackson (b. 1958), U.S. pop singer
In response to a cascade of press insinuations about the singer's sex life (including one story claiming that he'd had a romantic fling with Boy George), Jackson's manager held a national press conference in 1984 to refute widespread rumors that Jackson is a homosexual. Said Jackson in a printed statement distributed to reporters: "NO! I've never taken hormones to maintain my high voice. NO! I've never had my cheekbones altered in any way. NO! I've never had cosmetic surgery on my eyes. YES! One day in the future I plan to get married and have a family. Any statements to the contrary are simply untrue.... We all know that kids are very impressionable and therefore susceptible to such stories. I'm certain that some have already been hurt by this terrible slander. In addition to their admiration, I would like to keep their respect." Jackson threatened to sue any periodical that printed "new fantasies." Michael's brother Jermaine told one newspaper, "Even to say that he's not [gay] gives people the idea that he is. People want to hear ugliness." Jackson's publicist added, "If little girls want to grow up and marry Michael, now they know they've got a chance." The *Los Angeles Times* later commented: "There does not appear to be any precedent for a celebrity going to such lengths to proclaim his or her heterosexuality."

7. Richard Gere (b. 1950), U.S. actor
In 1994 Gere and his wife, supermodel Cindy Crawford, bought a $30,000 full-page ad in the London *Times* to refute rumors they are gay and had a marriage of convenience. "We got married because we love each other and we decided to make a life together," read the ad. "We are heterosexual and monogamous and take our commitment to each other very seriously." Gere told an interviewer in *Vanity Fair,* "The accusation is meaningless, and whether it's true or false is no one's business. I know who I am...." He told the Associated Press, "It's kid stuff. Kids in a schoolyard." Gere and Crawford were separated later that year.

8. **Christian Slater (b. 1969), U.S. actor**
In 1994 the actor—who has at various times been romantically linked with actress Winona Ryder and model Christy Turlington—denied rumors he is gay. "Being gay is not for me," he told *Playboy* magazine.

9. **Liberace (1919-1987), U.S. entertainer**
In 1959 Liberace sued the *London Daily Mirror* and one of its journalists for libel for implying that he was a homosexual. On the witness stand Liberace flatly denied he was a homosexual and stated he had never in his life indulged in homosexual practices. The trial lasted only six days, and Liberace won the suit and a $24,000 settlement. After Liberace died of AIDS complications in 1987, his homosexuality—an open secret within the entertainment industry—became widely known. The *London Daily Mirror* asked the entertainer's estate for its $24,000 back.

10. **John Travolta (b. 1954), U.S. actor**
Travolta was "outed" in a 1990 *National Enquirer* interview with fitness trainer and former Colt model Paul Barresi, who claimed to have had sex with the actor "dozens of times" after their initial meeting in the showers of a West Hollywood health club. Travolta angrily dismissed the allegation as "totally false" and told reporters, "I am not gay!" He became engaged to actress Kelly Preston seven months later. The two were married in the fall of 1991.

11. **Troy Donahue (b. 1936), U.S. actor**
Donahue told *People* magazine in 1984, "I am not gay. Once in a while people get me confused with another blond, blue-eyed actor who was around at the same time, but it's no big deal. I love women. Sometimes, I guess, too much." Donahue has been married four times, once to actress Suzanne Pleshette.

12. **Boy George (b. 1961), English pop singer**
The androgynous pop star told a London newspaper in 1984, "I'm not gay, and I'm not a transvestite, no matter what anybody thinks. I'm basically very much a man." At other times Boy George has

variously described himself as "bisexual," "very confused," "not confused," and "not really all that keen on sex." In recent years, however, he has finally acknowledged his homosexuality. "I have never penetrated a woman in my life," he has said.

13. **Randy Travis (b. 1963), U.S. country and western singer**
The popular singer angrily denied a 1991 supermarket tabloid story asserting that he is gay. "I usually let things slide," he said, "but I couldn't this time. There is not a man alive that can prove that statement, because it isn't true." Travis later joked, "I guess it could have been worse. They could've said I wasn't country."

14. **Rock Hudson (1925-1985), U.S. actor**
Hudson repeatedly denied rumors of his homosexuality, especially as they became more widespread during the last decade of his life. Even after acknowledging in 1985 that he was dying of AIDS complications, his spokeswoman initially told the press, "He doesn't have any idea how he contracted [it]." "Look, I know lots of gays in Hollywood," Hudson once told a reporter, "and most of them are nice guys. Some have tried it on with me, but I've said, 'Come on, now. You've got the wrong guy.'" Hudson rejected an offer to play Coach Brown in a film version of *The Front Runner* ("That's a totally unbelievable role for me," he protested) and was so concerned about the public's learning the truth about his private life that he never allowed reporters to photograph his gardens or the inside of his home for fear there might be visual clues to his homosexuality there.

15.-16. **Bert and Ernie**
In 1993 a traveling live show of *Sesame Street* characters was making a tour of the southern United States. After rumors began circulating in Mississippi that the puppets Bert and Ernie were not only homosexual but also actually married, ticket sales plummeted, and panicked parents inundated the offices of Jim Henson Productions with phone calls about the allegation. *Sesame Street* quickly issued a statement denying the gossip. The show's producers emphasized that Bert and Ernie were simply roommates.

3 Drag Ensembles Allegedly Worn by Former FBI Director J. Edgar Hoover

1. Short black dress, lace stockings, high heels, and false eyelashes (1958)

This outfit—described by one eyewitness as "fluffy"—was allegedly worn by Hoover in the spring of 1958 at a small private party at New York City's Plaza Hotel. Also in attendance were attorney Roy Cohn and two teenage boys with whom Hoover and Cohn later had sex. Hoover was also wearing makeup and garters. He went by the name "Mary Hoover."

2. "Roaring Twenties" red dress with opulent black feather boa (1959)

Hoover donned a flamboyant flapper-style dress, accentuating it with a lavish feather boa, for another party at the Plaza one year later. This time two leather boys also attended; Hoover allegedly made them read aloud from the Bible before he and repeat guest Roy Cohn initiated sex with them. Hoover's ensemble was described by an observer as "outlandish."

3. Evening gown, blond wig (1948)

Two men told Hoover biographer Anthony Summers that in 1948 they were shown pictures of the FBI director dressed as a woman. In the photographs Hoover was lying on a bed at a party, wearing an evening gown and a light-colored female wig. Said one of the men who viewed the photos, "Hoover made an ugly-looking woman."

NOTE: During his nearly fifty-year reign as FBI director, Hoover (1895-1972) became one of the most feared and powerful political figures in Washington. Ardently conservative and morally zealous, Hoover at first upgraded the FBI's image and efficiency, but then later corrupted its credibility with his often capricious and vicious vendettas against personal enemies or public figures whose politics or lifestyles he abhorred. He kept lengthy (and much feared) files on his enemies' private lives, including their sexual habits. His close 44-year friendship with constant companion Clyde Tolson, the number-two man at the FBI, aroused speculation about both men's sexuality, and Hoover often ruthlessly used his position to punish or threaten anyone he learned had spread gossip about them or had even hinted they were gay. Only recently has evidence of Hoover's homosexuality (and his occasional transvestism) been uncovered; the accounts above came from the best-selling biography *Official and Confidential: The Secret Life of J. Edgar Hoover* by Anthony Summers (Putnam, 1993).

10 Famous Gay Men and the Length of the FBI's Secret Surveillance File on Each

	Number of file pages
1. James Baldwin, U.S. author	1,302
2. Leonard Bernstein, U.S. composer/conductor	666
3. Truman Capote, U.S. author	185
4. Thornton Wilder, U.S. author	98
5. Andy Warhol, U.S. artist	71
6. W. H. Auden, British-U.S. poet	28
7. Jean Genet, French author	25
8. Tennessee Williams, U.S. playwright	7
9. Rock Hudson, U.S. actor	2
10. Allen Ginsberg, U.S. poet	1,000+

NOTE: Ginsberg's files have not been completely released, but at last count he had acquired, through the Freedom of Information Act, a "three-foot stack" of government documents on himself. The FBI has also kept files on Harvey Milk, Gore Vidal, E.M. Forster,

Christopher Isherwood, Harry Hay, Benjamin Britten, and countless other gay men as well as on numerous gay organizations ranging from SAGE (Senior Action in a Gay Environment) to ACT UP.

10 U.S. Police Departments That Have Actively Recruited Gay Men and Lesbians

1. San Francisco
2. Atlanta
3. Minneapolis
4. Seattle
5. Portland, Oregon
6. Boston
7. Madison, Wisconsin
8. Philadelphia
9. New York City
10. Los Angeles

7 Famous Gay Men Who Served in the U.S. Navy

1. Craig Claiborne (b. 1920), *New York Times* food critic
2. Rick Donovan (b. 1963), porn star
3. Allan Gurganus (b. 1947), writer
4. Rock Hudson (1925-1985), actor
5. Armistead Maupin (b. 1944), writer
6. Harvey Milk (1930-1978), politician and gay rights activist
7. Frank O'Hara (1926-1966), poet

2 Famous Gay Men Who Served in the U.S. Air Force

1. Leonard Matlovich (1943-1988), gay rights activist
2. Larry Townsend (b. 1935), writer

17 Famous Gay or Bisexual Men Who Served in the U.S. Army

1. Samuel Barber (1910-1981), composer
2. James Beard (1903-1985), food connoisseur and writer
3. William S. Burroughs (b. 1913), writer
4. John Cheever (1912-1982), writer
5. George Cukor (1899-1983), film director
6. Malcolm Forbes Sr. (1919-1990), businessman and magazine publisher
7. Andrew Holleran (b. 1946), writer
8. James Ivory (b. 1928), film director
9. Larry Kramer (b. 1935), writer
10. Rod McKuen (b. 1933), poet
11. James Merrill (1926-1995), poet
12. Merle Miller (1919-1986), writer
13. Peter Orlovsky (b. 1933), poet
14. Rev. Troy Perry (b. 1940), founder Metropolitan Community Church
15. John Rechy (b. 1934), writer
16. Gore Vidal (b. 1925), writer
17. Dr. Tom Waddell (1937-1987), decathlon athlete and gay rights activist

3 Famous Gay or Bisexual Men Who Served in the U.S. Marines

1. Dave Connors (1945-1985), porn star
2. Tyrone Power (1913-1958), actor
3. Oliver Sipple (1942-1989), gay ex-Marine who thwarted the 1975 assassination attempt by Sara Jane Moore on President Ford in San Francisco

14 Countries That Do Not Restrict Gays From Serving in the Military

1. Israel
2. Germany
3. Australia
4. Japan
5. France
6. The Netherlands
7. Sweden
8. Canada
9. Norway
10. Denmark
11. Ireland
12. Belgium
13. Austria
14. Spain

7 Supposed References to Homosexuality in the Bible (King James Version)

1. Leviticus 18:22
"Thou shalt not lie with mankind, as with womankind: it is abomination."

2. Leviticus 20:13
"If a man also lie with mankind, as he lieth with a woman, both of them have committed an abomination: they shall surely be put to death; their blood shall be upon them."

3. Deuteronomy 23:17
"There shall be no whore of the daughters of Israel, nor a sodomite of the sons of Israel."

4. I Kings 14:24
"And there were also sodomites in the land: and they did according to all the abominations of the nations which the Lord cast out before the children of Israel."

5. Romans 1:26-27
"For this cause God gave them up unto vile affections: for even their women did change the natural use into that which is against nature: And likewise also the men, leaving the natural use of the woman, burned in their lust one towards another; men with men working that which is unseemly, and receiving in themselves that recompense of their error which was meet."

6. Corinthians 6:9-10
"Know ye not that the unrighteous shall not inherit the kingdom of God? Be not deceived: neither fornicators, nor idolators, nor adulterers, nor effeminate, nor abusers of themselves with

mankind, Nor thieves, nor covetous, nor drunkards, nor revilers, nor extortioners shall inherit the kingdom of God."

7. I Timothy 1:9-10
"Knowing this, that the law is not made for a righteous man, but for the lawless and disobedient, for the ungodly and for sinners, for unholy and profane, for murderers of fathers and murderers of mothers, for manslayers, For whoremongers, for them that defile themselves with mankind, for menstealers, for liars, for perjured persons, and if there be any other thing that is contrary to sound doctrine."

NOTE: John Boswell's book *Christianity, Social Tolerance, and Homosexuality* (University of Chicago Press, 1980) makes an in-depth study of the likelihood that supposed condemnations of homosexuality in the Bible do not exist in the original texts at all but are actually the result of later translators imposing the prejudices of their times onto the translations. Boswell has written, "In spite of misleading English translations which may imply the contrary, the word 'homosexual' does not occur in the Bible: no extant text or manuscript, Hebrew, Greek, Syriac, or Aramaic, contains such a word.... There are of course ways to get around the lack of a specific word in a language, and an action may be condemned without being named, but it is doubtful in this particular case whether a concept of homosexual behavior as a class existed at all."

11 Admonitions in Leviticus That Fundamentalists Often Conveniently Forget About

1. Death penalty for using the Lord's name in vain
"He who blasphemes the name of the Lord shall be put to death; all the congregation shall stone him; the sojourner as well as the

native, when he blasphemes the Name, shall be put to death." (Lev. 24:16)

2. Prohibition against eating pork
"And the swine, because it parts the hoof and is cloven-footed but does not chew the cud, is unclean to you. Of their flesh you shall not eat, and their carcasses you shall not touch; they are unclean to you." (Lev. 11:7-8)

3. Mandating of animal sacrifices
"If anyone sins unwittingly in any of the things which the Lord has commanded not to be done, and does any one of them, if it is the anointed priest who sins, thus bringing guilt on the people, then let him offer for the sin which he has committed a young bull without blemish to the Lord as a sin offering. He shall bring the bull to the door of the tent of meeting before the Lord, and lay his hand on the head of the bull, and kill the bull before the Lord.... And all the fat of the bull of the sin offering he shall take from it, the fat that covers the entrails and all the fat that is on the entrails, and the two kidneys with the fat that is on them at the loins, and the appendage of the liver which he shall take away with the kidneys...and the priest shall burn them upon the altar...." (Lev. 4:1-10) [NOTE: The first several chapters of Leviticus are devoted to mandatory animal sacrifices, such as the wringing of turtledoves' necks, the cutting open of goats and bulls, and the vivisection of female lambs, for various sins.]

4. Death penalty for spiritualists
"A man or woman who is a medium or a wizard shall be put to death; they shall be stoned with stones, their blood shall be upon them." (Lev. 20:27)

5. Human slavery sanctioned
"As for your male and female slaves whom you may have: you may buy male and female slaves from among the nations that are round about you. You may also buy from among the strangers who sojourn with you and their families that are with you, who have

been born in your land; and they may be your property. You may bequeath them to your sons after you, to inherit as a possession for ever." (Lev. 25:44-46)

6. Prohibition against eating fat
"It shall be a perpetual statute throughout your generations, in all your dwelling places, that you eat neither fat nor blood." (Lev. 3:17)

7. Forbidding of hair and beard trimming
"You shall not round off the hair on your temples or mar the edges of your beard." (Lev. 19:27)

8. Prohibition against eating crab, clams, oysters
"Everything in the waters that has fins and scales, whether in the seas or in the rivers, you may eat. But anything in the seas or the rivers that has not fins and scales, of the swarming creatures in the waters and of the living creatures that are in the waters, is an abomination to you. They shall remain an abomination to you; of their flesh you shall not eat, and their carcasses you shall have in abomination. Everything in the waters that has not fins and scales is an abomination to you." (Lev. 11:9-12)

9. Death penalty for adultery
"If a man commits adultery with the wife of his neighbor, both the adulterer and the adulteress shall be put to death." (Lev. 20:10) [Leviticus lists four other kinds of adultery for which the death penalty is also mandatory.]

10. The profanity of disabled individuals
"For no one who has a blemish shall draw near, a man blind or lame, or who has a mutilated face or a limb too long, or a man who has an injured foot or an injured hand, or a hunchback, or a dwarf, or a man with a defect in his sights or an itching disease or scabs or crushed testicles; no man of the descendants of Aaron the priest who has a blemish shall come near to offer the Lord's offerings by fire; since he has a blemish, he shall not come near to offer the bread of his God.... He shall not come near the veil or approach

the altar, because he has a blemish, that he may not profane my sanctuaries...." (Lev. 21:18-23)

11. Other prohibitions
"You shall not let your cattle breed with a different kind; you shall not sow your field with two kinds of seed; nor shall there come upon you a garment of cloth made of two kinds of stuff." (Lev. 19:19)

The Gospel According to Pat: 12 Stupefying Quotes From the Rev. Pat Robertson

1. AIDS
"If, say, we're in a room with twenty-five people with AIDS and they're breathing various things into the atmosphere, the chance of somebody catching it has become quite strong."

2. Feminism
"Feminism...encourages women to leave their husbands, kill their children, practice witchcraft, destroy capitalism, and become lesbians."

3. Murder as an act of salvation
"God told the Israelites to kill them all [the Midianites], men, women, and children, to destroy them, and that seems a terrible thing to do. Is it? Well, that would be ten thousand people who probably would have gone to Hell. But if they stayed and reproduced...then there would be one million people who would have to spend eternity in Hell.... So, God in love, and that was a loving thing, took away a small number so that He might not have to take away a large number."

4. How he diverted a hurricane from his corporate headquarters in Virginia

"Word reached us that a great killer hurricane with winds exceeding one hundred fifty miles per hour was heading directly into our area.... I commanded that storm, in the name of Jesus, to stop its forward movement and to head back where it had come from.... It was almost as though a giant hand had come down out of the sky, blocked that storm, and gestured 'Stop!' This hurricane followed orders."

5. In response to a television producer who had publicly criticized him

"You are not merely trying to silence a member of the press, you are trying to silence a prophet of God.... The suppression of the voice of God's servant is a terrible thing. God Himself will fight for me against you—and He will win."

6. Who should be allowed to run for public office in the United States

"Individual Christians are the only ones really, and Jewish people.... Anyone whose mind and heart is not controlled by God Almighty is not qualified."

7. Drug abuse

"We have people today who have become slaves to a plant. Cannabis is a plant. So-called Mary Jane, marijuana, is a plant. People are slaves to a plant! Cocoa, cocaine, the coca plant—people are hooked on a vegetable!"

8. The origins of homosexuality

"I know a homosexual teacher in the place where I went to college. He was trying to have homosexual relations with various students, and I understand about thirty-five percent, thirty-six percent of all the homosexuals in America say that somehow they began this because of an adult who got them involved in it when they were children."

9. The establishment of a government religion
"The First Amendment says…Congress can't set up a national religion. End of story. There is never in the Constitution, at any point, anything that applies to the states. None at all."

10. Who his followers obey
"There is one ruler over the affairs of man—God Almighty. The Congress and the President are secondary to us."

11. The U.S. Constitution
"The Constitution of the United States…is a marvelous document for self-government by Christian people. But the minute you turn the document into the hands of non-Christians and atheistic people, they can use it to destroy the very foundation of your society."

12. On the coming religious and cultural war in America
"The strategy needed for Christian conservatives will resemble in part that of Douglas MacArthur in his campaign against the Japanese in the Pacific. Christians must take all the territory that is available with minimal struggle, then surround and isolate each stronghold and prepare to blast the enemy out of its position."

NOTE: A televangelist and multimillionaire businessman, Robertson ran for the Republican presidential nomination in 1988. Although unsuccessful, he scored several surprising political victories, including finishing second, ahead of George Bush, in the Iowa caucuses. Founder of the Christian Broadcasting Network (which changed its name to the more benign-sounding "Family Channel" in 1989), Robertson cohosts the widely seen 700 Club, on which he regularly denounces liberals, pro-choice advocates, civil libertarians, the media, feminists, secular theologians, homosexuals, and the so-called "gay agenda." He is one of the founders of the Christian Coalition, which actively assists conservative Christians in their battle against gay rights across the country. Although he has scaled back his personal political aspirations since 1988, he and his followers enjoy a significant influence within the Republican Party, and Robertson sees himself, not without reason, as a potential kingmaker in any Republican campaign for the presidency.

29 Famous People Who Had Gay or Bisexual Sons

1. Lady Nancy Astor (1879-1964), British stateswoman
2. Marcus Aurelius (121-180), Roman emperor and philosopher
3. Josephine Baker (1906-1975), U.S. singer and dancer
4. Catherine de' Medici (1519-1589), queen of France
5. Anthony Eden (1897-1977), British prime minister
6. Edward I (1239-1307), king of England
7. Eleanor of Aquitaine (1122-1204), queen of England
8. Frederick Wilhelm I (1688-1740), king of Prussia
9. Elliott Gould (b. 1938), U.S. actor
10. Robert Guillaume (b. 1937), U.S. actor
11. Henry II (1133-1189), king of England
12. Laura Z. Hobson (1900-1986), U.S. writer
13. Russell Johnson (b. 1925), "The Professor" on TV's *Gilligan's Island*
14. Stanley Kramer (b. 1913), U.S. film director
15. Alfred Krupp (1812-1887), German munitions manufacturer
16. Tommy Lasorda (b. 1927), U.S. baseball manager
17. Roy Lichtenstein (b. 1923), U.S. painter
18. Louis XIII (1601-1643), king of France
19. Robert MacNeil (b. 1931), Canadian-U.S. television news anchor
20. Mary, Queen of Scots (1542-1587)
21. Joseph Papp (1921-1991), U.S. theatrical producer
22. Philip II (382-336 B.C.), Macedonian king
23. Ptolemy III (266-221 B.C.), king of Egypt
24. Oral Roberts (b. 1918), U.S. evangelist
25. Edmond Rostand (1868-1918), French playwright
26. Phyllis Schlafly (b. 1924), U.S. conservative activist
27. Barbra Streisand (b. 1942), U.S. entertainer
28. William the Conqueror (1027-1087), king of England
29. Loretta Young (b. 1913), U.S. actress

3 Famous Men Who Had Gay Grandsons

1. Chester Arthur (1830-1886), U.S. president
2. Ernest Hemingway (1899-1961), U.S. writer
3. Barry Goldwater (b. 1909), U.S. senator

Dr. James Packer's 6 Signs Your Son May Be Turning Into a Homosexual

1. "Feminine touches in your son's clothing. Soft, clingy fabrics and pale, girlish colors are definite warning signals."
2. "A boy who hangs out indoors and reads.... If your son is reading something romantic, like *Gone With the Wind,* he's probably teetering on the verge of homosexuality."
3. "If your son is bringing home 'buddies' who wear earrings, tight T-shirts, or heavy perfumes. And, of course, if he's hanging out with male flight attendants."
4. "If your kid doesn't like sports or chooses hobbies like knitting or flower arranging."
5. "Listening to classical pieces [of music] or recordings of Liberace."
6. "If your son usually hangs out with guys and avoids dating."

NOTE: Dr. Packer, a South African sociologist, has said, "I never thought my boy was in danger until I took a close look at him and realized he was listening to classical music.... My son denied it, but I knew he was heading toward a strange love life and a future as a hairdresser or ballet dancer. Luckily, I caught it in time."

SOURCE: "How to Tell If Your Son Is Gay" by Dorothy Steele. *World Weekly News*: December 8, 1992

5 Men Who Were Raised As Girls

1. Ernest Hemingway (1899-1961), U.S. writer

Family friends speculated that Grace Hemingway never wanted a boy and that was why she kept Ernest dressed as a girl during so much of his youth. Whether Grace really objected to his gender is open to debate, but she did make her son wear girls' clothing during the first five years of his life, and she styled his hair in feminine bangs and long pretty curls. She adoringly referred to him as her "Dutch dolly" and enjoyed having him photographed in lacy pink dresses and wide flowered hats. By the time he was three, little Ernest openly worried how Santa Claus would ever know he was a boy. His older sister, Marcelline, meanwhile, was held back a year from starting kindergarten so that she and Ernest could attend their first classes together as twin little girls.

All of this gender confusion probably added to the bitter resentment Hemingway felt toward his mother throughout much of his life. "I hate her guts, and she hates mine," he once told his publisher, Charles Scribner. He was so embarrassed about his childhood that even when he was fifty he threatened to cut off all financial support to his elderly mother if she ever revealed the details of his boyhood to interviewers.

2. Robert Peary (1856-1920), U.S. explorer

The Arctic explorer, traditionally credited with leading the first expedition to the North Pole, was raised in an era when mothers frequently dressed their infant sons as girls. However, even by Victorian standards, Peary's mother—a lonely widow who doted on her only child—was excessive. She dressed young Robert—whom she nicknamed "Bertie"—as a girl long after his infancy. She also fussed endlessly over his beautiful skin, forced him to wear a woman's sunbonnet whenever he went outside, and made him learn lace-making and other handicrafts reserved at the time for genteel young ladies. By the time he attended school he had developed a severe lisp and was constantly taunted and physically assaulted by his classmates. Peary's biographers have speculated that his "peculiar" childhood as well as the drubbing he received from his boyhood peers fueled much of his fierce ambition later in life.

3. Douglas MacArthur (1880-1964), U.S. military leader
MacArthur's mother, Pinky, dressed him as a girl for the first eight years of life. An assertive but unhappy woman, she worried that he might become too independent, and he remained utterly dominated by her throughout most of his youth. She kept him dressed in long skirts and pretty feathered hats or made him wear dresses with big colorful bows. He was also made to wear his hair in long, elegant, feminine curls until shortly before the onset of puberty. Later in life, after MacArthur had achieved fame and respect in the military, a friend nicknamed him "Sarah" (after French actress Sarah Bernhardt) because of his vanity and love of costumes and military finery.

4. Thomas Wolfe (1900-1938), U.S. writer
Wolfe was the youngest of seven children, and his mother, Julia—a repressed and bitter woman—liked to boast, "He being the baby, I kept him a baby." Not only did she sleep with him until he was six, but she also continued to breast-feed him until he was almost four. She curled his hair every day and made it look so unabashedly feminine that his schoolmates accused him of being a girl. (Young Thomas pulled down his pants to prove them wrong.) It wasn't until he caught a severe case of head lice at the age of nine that his mother relented and finally allowed him to wear his hair short as other boys did.

5. Rainer Maria Rilke (1875-1926), German poet
Having lost an infant daughter just twelve months earlier, Rilke's mother, Sophie, was bitterly disappointed when she gave birth to a son in 1875. Until Rilke was seven years old, his mother steadfastly refused, in the words of one biographer, "to acknowledge his

gender." She forced him to wear lavish dresses, kept his blond hair long and beautifully curled, and gave him dolls and other typically feminine toys to play with. Rilke resented his mother all his life. He once complained that the only time she ever paid any attention to him in his youth was "when there was a chance to present me in a new little dress to a few admiring friends."

8 Famous Gay Men Who Also Had a Gay Brother

1. Sir Francis Bacon (1561-1626), English philosopher and statesman

Both Francis and his older brother, Anthony, were gay. The two were devoted to one another as boys and remained close throughout their lives. In fact, they lived together for a time, and it was to his "loving and beloved Brother" that Francis dedicated his famous *Essays* in 1597. Their mother—domineering, intelligent, and devoutly religious—was well aware of their sexual inclinations and sent them both a stream of letters anxiously lecturing them about their health and their souls as well as their choice of bed partners. Sending an errand boy with strawberries to them one morning, she told them pointedly that the strawberries were theirs to keep, the errand boy was not. On another occasion she sternly lectured Francis about "that bloody Percy," a man Francis was keeping as "coach companion and bed companion."

Anthony's sexual adventures eventually led him to be arrested and charged with sodomy in France in 1590. Fortunately, his friend Henry of Navarre—then king—intervened, and the impending sentence of death was suspended. After a long history of physical ailments (neither brother had a strong constitution), Anthony died in 1601 from gout at the age of 42. His brother lived on for another quarter of a century.

2. Francois Duquesnoy (1597-1643), Flemish sculptor
The Duquesnoy brothers, Francois and Jerome, came from a family of famous artists and were themselves both noted sculptors during the early seventeenth century. They were also both homosexuals. Francois, the older and better known of the two, died in 1643. Eleven years later, Jerome—whose work included commissions for Philip IV of Spain and the empress of Russia—was arrested in Ghent, in northern Belgium, for allegedly sodomizing two of his young male models. Despite his official standing as a court sculptor at Flanders and despite the pleas of highly placed friends, including the Bishop of Trieste, he was condemned to die. On September 28, 1654, by order of the court, he was lashed to a stake, strangled to death, and his body then burned.

3. Frederick the Great (1712-1786), king of Prussia
Frederick had a younger brother, Henry, prince of Prussia, of whom he was enormously fond. Henry, like Frederick, was gay. Henry was fourteen years younger, and Frederick personally supervised his education, making certain he received a broad, liberal background in history and the arts and sciences. Later, as a young general commanding troops in the Seven Years War, Henry performed ably in Frederick's name. In the U.S. during the late 1700s, when consideration was being given to substituting the fledgling democracy with a constitutional monarchy, Alexander Hamilton and James Monroe, among others, suggested Henry as a candidate for the United States' first king.

4. Peter Ilyich Tchaikovsky (1840-1893), Russian composer
The composer's brother Modeste was also gay.

5. A.E. Housman (1859-1936), English poet
Housman had not only a gay brother—noted playwright Laurence Housman—but also a lesbian sister.

6. Constantine Cavafy (1863-1933), Greek poet
The youngest of eight children, Cavafy's older brother Paul was also gay. However, because of differences in their characters—Con-

stantine was pampered, introspective, obsessed with ancient history and poetry; Paul was something of an opportunist and social gadfly who spent much of his life in debt—the two were never particularly close.

7. Charles Laughton (1899-1962), British actor
Laughton's younger brother Frank, a renowned chef, was also gay. He died a year after Laughton.

8. Jeff Stryker (b. 1966), U.S. porn star
Stryker has a bisexual brother, Rick, who has also appeared in gay porn films, including *Every Which Way* and *Powerfull II.* "Yes, he's my real brother," Stryker has said, "but the only place he looks like me is his dick." When asked if he had any qualms about his brother being in porn, Stryker replied, "I'd rather have him making movies than selling dope or stealing. This is an honest way to make a living, and you're doing a service for people."

NOTE: According to a 1986 study at Boston University's School of Medicine, gay men are five times more likely than heterosexual men to have a gay brother.

10 Most Common Explanations for Why People Are Gay

1. Homosexuality is a genetic trait. It is hereditary and passed on from one generation to the next.

2. Men who become homosexuals were raised in families where the mother was dominant or smothering and the father was weak or indifferent.

3. Homosexuality is a natural sexual impulse within all of us; because of various complex circumstances, certain individuals simply express it more than other individuals.

4. Experienced adult homosexuals actively recruit young people to become gay, either through seduction or molestation.

5. Homosexuality is caused by hormone imbalances. Male homosexuals have unusually high levels of estrogen—a female sex hormone—in their systems. (Other theories claim that gay men have too much androgen, a male sex hormone, in their systems.)

6. A child raised or treated as a member of the opposite sex will become a homosexual: For example, a little boy dressed up as a girl or given a doll to play with is more likely to grow up gay.

7. Social or legal acceptance of homosexuality leads to its spread. For instance, if young people see homosexuality accepted all around them, they'll think it's okay to be gay and are more likely to become homosexuals themselves.

8. People become homosexuals because they are too unattractive or too shy to make it with the opposite sex. Also, men with small penises become homosexuals because they're afraid to have sex with women.

9. People turn to homosexuality because of a traumatic sexual experience with the opposite sex.

10. Boys grow up to be homosexuals because of guilt feelings or "castration anxiety" associated with having intercourse with women.

11 Memorable Suspected Causes of Homosexuality

1. Loud disco music
A 1979 study at Aegean University in Turkey alleged that male mice continually exposed to loud disco music eventually became exclusively homosexual. The university claimed to have discovered that "high-level noise, such as that frequently found in discos, causes homosexuality in mice and deafness among pigs."

2. Home economics class
In 1974 two Baptist ministers in Milford, Connecticut, became enraged when the local school board made home economics a required course for sixth-grade boys. "By having a young boy cook or sew, wearing aprons, we're pushing a boy into homosexuality," complained one of the ministers. Said the other, "My son doesn't want the course, and I don't want him to be a sissy." They demanded, unsuccessfully, that the board reverse itself.

3. Automobile accidents
In 1976 a Detroit jury awarded more than $200,000 in damages to a man who contended he was "turned into" a homosexual by a recent automobile accident. The man's car had, perhaps appropriately, been rear-ended by another vehicle.

4. Smoking marijuana

In 1986 Reagan-appointed White House drug adviser Carlton Turner announced his belief that smoking marijuana leads to homosexuality. Turner claimed that when he visited treatment centers for drug abusers under eighteen, he found that approximately forty percent of the patients had also engaged in homosexual activity. "It seems to be something that follows along from their marijuana use," he told the press. Similar assertions had been made in 1979 by then-U.S. senator S.I. Hayakawa (R-Calif.), who claimed that a widespread use of marijuana was responsible for the "huge increase" in homosexuality.

5. Astrological influences

The 1933 book *Strange Loves* by Dr. La Forest Potter devoted an entire section to the question "Are astrological factors in any way accountable for perversion?" "There may be something more than mere coincidence," Dr. Potter concluded, "in the fact that many persons, born under certain aspects, seem to develop sexual abnormalities. In this respect one born under the sign Libra—the balances—seems to be more than usually vulnerable." Some ancient Greeks and Romans also believed that astrology played an important part in determining sexual preference.

6. Hard-core pornography

In his 1970 book *Changing Homosexuality in the Male,* New York psychiatrist Lawrence Hatterer denounced what he called the "homosexualization" of America and put much of the blame on the burgeoning "hard-core homosexual pornography industry." Hatterer suggested that the stimulating nature of such films pushed otherwise "healthy" young heterosexual males "over the line" into perversion.

7. Masturbation

During the Victorian era, masturbation was popularly thought to lead inevitably to homosexual behavior. "Typical" young male masturbators were often portrayed in medical literature as having effeminate mannerisms and developing "morbid attachments" to other boys or young men.

8. Vasectomy
In 1981 British medical researchers reported the case of a 32-year-old married man who became exclusively homosexual after undergoing a vasectomy. The man claimed to have had no previous homosexual experiences.

9. Too many female teachers
One early twentieth-century theory suggested that young boys whose grade school teachers were mostly women were more likely to become homosexuals.

10. Atavism
Another early theory claimed that homosexuals were genetic throwbacks to the human race's primitive and amoral ancestors. Some scientists thought they saw this substantiated by the high degree of homosexual behavior among so-called lesser animals, including various apes.

11. Uncut meat
An aboriginal society in New Guinea believes that men will become homosexuals if they eat the meat of uncircumcised pigs.

12 Alleged Cures for Homosexuality

1. Aversion therapy
The administration of strong drugs or electric shock in order to condition a person to associate homosexuality with fear and pain. While being shown sexually arousing homosexual scenes, the patient is rendered acutely ill by electric shocks, emetics, or drugs that induce a feeling of suffocation or drowning.

2. Castration

Removal of the testicles and/or the penis in order to destroy sexual desire and functioning. Castration was sometimes used in mental hospitals as a treatment for homosexuality and "habitual" masturbation. It was also used as medical treatment or court-ordered punishment for men convicted of so-called homosexual sex crimes. As late as the 1950s, castration was still seen as a legitimate subject for research into curing homosexuality in the U.S.

3. Diet therapy

The regulation of diet, nutrition, and bodily metabolism in order to control and eradicate homosexual impulses. For example, one theory held that homosexuality was caused by constipation, flatulence, or other bowel irritations that could be relieved with the proper diet. Another theory proposed that homosexuality was caused by bladder irritations, which could be relieved by eliminating fish and certain other foods from one's meals. Macrobiotics, vegetarianism, megavitamin therapy, vegetotherapy, and other specialized diets have all had their adherents as "cures."

4. Drug therapy

The injection of everything from pulverized lamb embryos to LSD. In the case of English mathematician Alan Turing, convicted of "gross indecencies" with another male in 1952 and ordered to undergo therapy for his homosexuality, the drug was estrogen—female sex hormone—administered to curb his libido. (Among the side effects: Turing suffered impotence, depression, and the growth of feminine breasts. He killed himself shortly after completing the treatment.) Sexual stimulants and depressants as well as strong general sedatives such as Thorazine have also been used to try to cure homosexuality.

5. "The love of a good woman"

Heterosexual marriage, or intercourse with a woman, are still often regarded as cures for homosexuality. In one of the more memorable failures, poet Ernest Dowson took Oscar Wilde to a French brothel to cure Wilde of his homosexuality after he was released from prison.

"The first these ten years," Wilde said of his heterosexual experience, "and it will be the last. It was like cold mutton!" In the 1960s three physicians tried one cure known as the "Masturbation Method": Homosexuals were told to masturbate in an assigned darkened room, and at the moment of orgasm, lights came on illuminating graphic pictures of naked women. It was hoped that the patients would learn to associate orgasmic pleasure with the opposite sex.

6. Lobotomy

A form of psychosurgery involving cutting into the brain and severing nerve fibers. Lobotomies were performed as late as the 1950s to "cure" homosexuality. State hospitals routinely performed the operation to control "serious management problems," which often included homosexuals or so-called compulsive masturbators. Between 1940 and 1955, some 50,000 prefrontal lobotomies were performed in the United States. Many of these patients were left in a near-vegetative condition. As late as 1970, a Dr. Fritz Roeder announced that he had "cured" homosexuals as well as exhibitionists and transvestites by performing surgery on their brains and destroying part of the hypothalamus gland with electricity. "Young homosexual men," he wrote, "most of them pedophiliacs, are promptly transformed into the straight world."

7. Physical therapy

Rectal and prostate massage. According to some theories, prostate massage kills the "homosexual cells" in the prostate and replaces them with "healthy, heterosexual cells."

8. Radiation therapy

Doses of X-ray radiation administered to various glands in the body in order to alter the functioning of those glands. This was used by doctors who suspected homosexuality of being caused by hormone imbalances or other metabolic dysfunctions.

9. Anaphrodisiac therapy

The administration of substances alleged to diminish the sex drive and the use of various physical devices in order to impair or destroy sexual interest. This has included the use of ice cold baths and penis cages and the oral administration of saltpeter and cod liver oil.

10. Shock treatment

Electrically or chemically induced shock and convulsions. In the 1930s, experiments to find a cure for homosexuality involved pharmacological shock treatment: inducing grand mal seizures in homosexuals by giving them massive overdoses of drugs.

11. **Torture, exorcism, and death**

Torture and exorcism have both been used to "cure" homosexuality. Burning at the stake, hanging, and strangulation were often seen by religious authorities not as punishments for homosexuality but as cures, since they allegedly released a homosexual from the torments of the flesh and prevented him from committing further sins.

12. Gene therapy

The administration of drugs or the introduction into the body of gene-altering material in order to turn off a "gay gene," if one exists. Some researchers have predicted that if homosexuality is hereditary, the gene or group of genes responsible will be isolated and a method for altering them will emerge soon afterward. Homosexuality might also then be detected in the womb, through a simple genetic test, and prospective parents would presumably be given options to abort the fetus, alter the sexual orientation of the unborn child, or proceed with the pregnancy without tampering.

Dr. La Forest Potter's 10 Characteristics of the Average Homosexual

1. Large, easily aroused nipples
2. Mincing walk
3. Sloped and rounded shoulders
4. Thick, "luxuriant" hair
5. Hairless chest
6. Soft, delicate skin ("…acne spots, so frequently present in normal men, are usually absent.")
7. A peculiar swinging motion of the hips (due to anatomical defects in the spine and pelvis)
8. Lack of willpower, perseverance, and "dogmatic energy"
9. A considerable deposit of fat in the region of the hips, breasts, and thighs
10. Abnormally wide hips, "feminine buttocks"

SOURCE: Dr. La Forest Potter, *Strange Loves: A Study in Sexual Abnormalities.* New York, The Robert Dodsley Company, 1933

8 Intriguing Scientific Speculations About Gay Men

1. Penis length

A 1970 study published in *Sexology* magazine concluded that gay men have larger penises than heterosexual men. The study found that the penises of homosexuals are an average of a third of an inch longer and .08 inch wider than those of heterosexual males. The measurements were for nonerect penises only.

2. Left-handedness
According to a Canadian study conducted at McMaster University in the 1980s, gay men are somewhat more likely, and lesbians almost twice as likely, to be either left-handed or ambidextrous, compared with the general population. The study seemed especially significant since handedness is a function of brain organization and is thought to be determined by prenatal hormone levels in the womb.

3. General attractiveness
A study conducted at the University of Toronto and published in the February 1993 issue of *Archives of Sexual Behavior* concluded that gay men are, on the whole, better-looking than heterosexual men. In the study, participants were asked to rate the faces of various test subjects (without knowledge of the subjects' backgrounds) on a scale from 1 to 5 in the categories of "handsome," "pretty," "cute," "beautiful," and "attractive."

4. Onset of puberty
A 1982 study found that homosexual men, on the whole, reach puberty and achieve secondary sex characteristics earlier than heterosexual men.

5. Testosterone levels
In the early 1970s researchers at the Masters and Johnson sex research institute in St. Louis concluded that homosexual men have lower levels of testosterone in their blood than heterosexual men. This contradicted a study from the '40s that found that some homosexual men have higher levels of testosterone in their blood as well as a study from the '60s that concluded homosexuals have the same levels of testosterone in their blood as heterosexual males. Some researchers have speculated that the discrepancies among the studies may be explained by a steadily increasing efficiency in the methods of measuring hormone levels in the blood. Others have discounted the idea that there are any differences in testosterone levels between homosexual and heterosexual men.

6. The suprachiasmatic nucleus

Dutch researchers at the Netherlands Institute for Brain Research found, in 1990, that homosexual men have a significantly larger suprachiasmatic nucleus in their brains than heterosexual men. The suprachiasmatic nucleus—which is known primarily as a regulator of the body's day/night rhythms—as yet has no known role in sexual behavior. However, the significance of the study lay primarily in discovering what may be the first known physiological difference between homosexuals and heterosexuals.

7. The hypothalamus

A 1991 Salk Institute study preliminarily suggested that the hypothalamus—a part of the brain believed to control male sexual behavior—is twice as large in heterosexual men as in homosexual men. Although it was impossible to draw definitive conclusions from the study, it did suggest new avenues of exploration for researchers studying a biological basis for homosexuality.

8. Gay relatives

In the early 1990s a study of the families of seventy-six male homosexuals found that maternal uncles and cousins of gay men are much more likely to also be gay than paternal uncles or cousins, suggesting to some that homosexuality, if confirmed to be a genetic trait, might be passed down through the mother.

7 Antiquated Medical Terms for "Homosexuality"

1. Homophilia
2. Similisexualism
3. Uranianism
4. Mental hermaphrodism
5. Homogenitalism
6. Intersexualism
7. Androgynism

16 Unusual or Archaic Expressions for "Gay Man"

1. Androgyne

Used as early as the 1500s to describe a hermaphrodite (a person born with both male and female sex organs), a eunuch, or an effeminate man; later, also a term for "homosexual." From the Greek *androgynos,* meaning literally "male and female in one."

2. Backgammon player

Eighteenth-century slang in reference to a male homosexual who enjoyed anal intercourse.

3. Bird

Originally, British slang for "female prostitute," but by the 1920s it also referred to a male homosexual or any person generally regarded as different or outrageous.

4. Buttercup

Early 1930s slang for "effeminate male homosexual."

5. Cornholer

Rural American slang for "gay man." From the days when dried corncobs were used for anal hygiene in the outhouse. Chiefly now, when used at all, a term among young adolescents.

6. Ganymede

"A boy kept for 'unnatural' purposes," or "a young man beloved by an older man." Also used during the High Middle Ages in reference to any gay male. In Greek mythology, the Trojan boy Ganymede was so beautiful that Zeus, the father of the gods, kidnapped him and made him his cupbearer and lover. (Later, ancient Roman mythology changed *Ganymede* to *Catamitus,* and *catamite* also became a term referring to a kept boy.)

7. Gentleman of the back door

Included in Captain Francis Grose's *Classical Dictionary of the Vulgar Tongue* (1785) as an eighteenth-century British slang term for "male homosexual." A variation was *usher of the back door.*

8. Gunsel

"A young, inexperienced male homosexual"; also, "the passive partner in anal intercourse." Derived from the German and Yiddish word *gaensel,* which was prison slang for "a passive boy kept by another inmate." In the film *The Maltese Falcon,* Humphrey Bogart calls Sydney Greenstreet's trigger-happy young companion, Wilmer, a gunsel, although by then the expression had also come to mean "a petty gangster or hoodlum."

9. Invert

Popular as a scientific or pseudoscientific term from the late 1800s up until about the 1940s. Homosexuality was often referred to as "inversion" or "the inverted sexual instinct."

10. Lizzie

Popular 1920s slang for "a male homosexual."

11. Molly

In London in the 1700s, there were various raucous men's clubs: the Blasters, the Bold Bucks, the Sweaters, and the Mollies. The Mollies, who probably took their name from a common term of the time for "female prostitutes," were widely known as homosexuals and were noted for their wild partying in women's clothing. The term *molly* eventually came to refer to any homosexual or effeminate man; a *molly house* was a house of prostitution that catered to homosexuals; and a *molly cot* was a prissy or unassertive male. To *mollycoddle* someone still means "to pamper them excessively, to the point of emasculation."

12. Nancy

Nancy was English slang for "buttocks" in the 1800s, but by the turn of the century it meant, on both sides of the Atlantic, "a homosexual or an effeminate man." Variations included *nancy boy* and *nance.*

13. 175-er

Popular in Germany as a pejorative for "gay man" during the 1920s and 1930s. Derived from Paragraph 175 of the German Penal Code, which mandated harsh criminal provisions for homosexual acts.

14. Pederast

From the Greek *paed,* meaning "boy," and *erastis,* meaning "lover"; hence, "a lover of boys." In 1613 English travel writer Samuel Purchas visited Sicily and wrote in his book *Pilgrimage,* "He telleth of their Paederastie, that they buy Boyes at a hundred or two hundred duckats, and mew them up for their filthie lust."

15. Tommy Dodd

Late-Victorian slang for "gay man." Gay men were sometimes referred to as "tommies."

16. Uranian

Coined in 1862 by German homosexual rights advocate Karl Heinrich Ulrichs, who took the term from Plato's *Symposium,* in which homosexual love was said to exist under the protection of the ninth muse, Urania. In the late 1800s German homosexuals frequently called themselves Uranians, and use of the term soon spread to other countries, including the United States. One early homosexual rights group used the slogan "Uranians of the World, Unite!"

5 Possible Origins for the Word "Faggot" as a Pejorative for "Gay Man"

1. Schoolboy sex slaves

In nineteenth-century English public schools, "fagging" was the system under which lowerclassmen were obliged to perform certain duties—such as polishing boots, running errands, or merely obeying whimsical orders—for the upperclassmen. The system was similar to hazing, though often crueler, and it had definite sexual overtones, since it was not uncommon for the younger boys to sexually service the seniors. For example, in his memoirs English writer John Addington Symonds noted that in his first year at public school, "every boy of good looks had a female name and was recognized either as a public prostitute or as some bigger fellow's 'bitch.'" To be one of these drudges or sexual lackeys was to be, in the slang of the day, a "fag." The current use of *fag* and *faggot* for "gay man" may be an extension of this earlier meaning.

2. Burning faggots

As far back as the fourteenth century, the word *faggot* referred to the bundle of sticks and twigs used as kindling for burning people—such as "sodomites" and "buggers"—at the stake. Some people now believe that the use of the word *faggot* as a pejorative for "gay man" originated with this medieval practice of executing homosexuals by burning.

3. Smoking faggots

In British slang around the time of World War I, cigarettes were often referred to as "fags." Despite their growing popularity at the time, they were frequently regarded as unmanly, especially compared to a cigar or a pipe, and men who smoked them were sometimes ridiculed as effeminate. As a result, in the popular mind cigarettes may have come to be identified with effeminacy and homosexuality, and gay men may have come to be called "fags" themselves.

4. Gay sorcerers

In her book *Another Mother Tongue,* poet and historian Judy Grahn suggests that gay men came to be called "faggots" because of the word's long mystical association with sacred fire and the sorcerer's wand. She writes: "The faggot as a wand for divination and sacred firemaking has apparently belonged to the province of Gay male wizards, sorcerers, and priests for thousands of years."

5. Disagreeable faggots

As far back as the 1500s, *faggot* has been a term of abuse or contempt applied to a disagreeable or objectionable woman. The term, in this context, may eventually have been applied to gay men, since homosexuals have often been seen in much the same contemptuous and abusive light as women and since they have also generally been regarded as disagreeable or objectionable.

14 Prominent People Who Have Publicly Referred to Gay Men as "Faggots" or "Fags"

1. Richard Armey, U.S. congressman (R-Texas)

Referred to gay congressman Barney Frank as "Barney Fag" during public remarks on the House floor in 1995.

2. John Wayne, actor

Complained, in a 1971 *Playboy* magazine interview, about the number of "perverted" movies being made and sarcastically referred to *Midnight Cowboy* as a "wonderful love story about two fags."

3. Tony Randall, actor
Told *After Dark* magazine in a 1972 interview that he'd recently gone with friends to a gay porn theater in Los Angeles. "Just terrible," he said of the experience. "Just disgusting. Guys sucking each other's cocks. There's nothing to watch in that. It confirms something I've always suspected about homosexuality—they don't like it. These guys never got aroused." In the same interview he asserted, "There is no such thing as homosexuality—it's just something invented by a bunch of fags."

4. Rush Limbaugh, conservative commentator
After the December 1990 Queer Nation protest at St. Patrick's Cathedral in New York City, he told his radio listeners, "I feel like doing this whole program with just one word: *faggie, faggie, faggie.*" "If you can't deal with the guilt of your own existence," he told homosexuals, "then it's time you sought comfort in the Church, rather than looking at it as the enemy."

5. Mort Sahl, Canadian-U.S. talk show host
Called for the execution of "faggots" and "homos" during a television panel discussion on feminism in 1975. Denounced gay people as "destructive...a negative social force." "They are the enemy!" he warned. He also characterized the American Civil Liberties Union as "lawyers for faggots."

6. Frank Rizzo, former mayor of Philadelphia
During his inauguration as mayor in 1972, he declared, "I'm gonna make Attila the Hun look like a faggot!"

7. Pauline Kael, film critic
In her 1970 *New Yorker* review of the film *The Boys in the Band,* she wrote: "In the theater, *The Boys in the Band* was a conventional play.... It was like *The Women,* but with a forties-movie bomber-crew cast: a Catholic, a Jew, a Negro, a butch faggot, a nellie faggot, a hustler, and so on.... The fun of the faggot vernacular and the interaction of the troupe of actors onstage helped a little to conceal the play's mechanics...." When the review was reprinted

three years later in her anthology *Deeper Into Movies,* all uses of the word *faggot* had been deleted.

8. Eddie Murphy, comic and actor
His 1983 HBO comedy special, *Delirious,* opened with a tirade against "faggots." After a string of jokes about AIDS, he then launched into a parody of *The Honeymooners* in which Ralph Kramden begged Norton to sodomize him. "Faggots aren't allowed to look at my ass while I'm onstage," Murphy told the audience. "I'm afraid of gay people. Petrified. I have nightmares about gay people." When he was later asked in *Rolling Stone* magazine about the criticism his routine generated, Murphy replied, "Faggots who have nothing to fucking do but sit around with tight asses and feel like people are pointing fingers at them...people who are insecure got offended."

9. Andrew Dice Clay, comic
Self-described as "the most vulgar, vicious comic ever to walk the face of the earth," Clay regularly referred to gays as "faggots," "queers," "homos," and "fruits" during his stand-up comedy routines during the late '80s.

10. David Hemmings, British actor
Publicly described his role as a gay man in the 1971 film *The Love Machine* as "a screaming faggot" and a "snarling fag."

11. Bill Maher, comic and talk-show host
Defending his heterosexuality during a 1995 interview with Camille Paglia on his TV show *Politically Incorrect,* he insisted, "When the waters of the sexual revolution started getting rough, you didn't see me swimming out to fag island!"

12. Richard Schickel, film critic
Regularly used the words *fag* and *faggot* (as well as *dyke*) in his film reviews during the '60s and '70s. His review of *Midnight Cowboy* contained a brief discussion of "faggery" in general, and he congratulated *The Killing of Sister George* on its depiction of the "fag" milieu.

13. Judy Klemesrud, entertainment reporter for *The New York Times*
In a 1968 feature story on *The Boys in the Band,* she described the character of Emory as a "pansy…the show's only swishy, 42nd Street stereotype fag."

14. Robert Mitchum, actor
Described himself in a 1983 *Esquire* interview as having been "a faggot's dream" in his youth and remarked, "I don't care what I play. I'll play Polish faggots, midgets, women, anything. Any role."

7 Famous Men Who Disliked the Word "Gay"

1. Truman Capote, (1924-1984), U.S. writer
Capote complained that the word *gay* was "inept and inaccurate" and confessed that he hated it. "I do wish they'd come up with something else," he told *Newsday* in 1978. "Even spell it backwards. Even *yags,* I think, would be better."

2. Paul Cadmus, (b. 1914), U.S. painter
In one of his rare interviews, Cadmus told *The Advocate* in 1976, "Maybe I shouldn't say this, it's a word that's used universally now, but the word *gay* doesn't please me. I think it sounds too frivolous. Think of calling Socrates gay or Michelangelo gay. Gaiety is a wonderful thing, but it does sound as though that were the whole aim in life, as though it were a career in itself. That depresses me a bit."

3. Gore Vidal, (b. 1925), U.S. writer
Vidal told the newspaper *Fag Rag* in 1974 that he had "never allowed, actively, in my life the word *gay* to pass my lips.… It's just a bad word. You see, I don't think you need a word for it. This is what you have to evolve. These words have got to wither away in a true Hegelian cycle."

4. Christopher Isherwood (1904-1986), British-U.S. writer
In 1975 Isherwood told *Advocate* interviewer W.I. Scobie that the word *gay* sounded "coy" to his "old-fashioned ears." "*Gay* is fine as a slogan," he said, "a watchword, a term to describe our philosophy, our attitude toward life. But not, I think, as a title for the movement. I prefer the words used by our enemies. I used to call myself a bugger when I was young. Now I feel at home with *queer* or *fag* when I'm feeling hostile. It makes heterosexuals wince when you refer to yourself by those words if they've been using them behind your back, as they generally have."

5. Franco Zeffirelli (b. 1923), Italian film director
Zeffirelli told one interviewer, "I hate to call certain human beings 'gay.' The moment you say 'gay,' I see already a movement or a category or a ghetto. I don't like that at all."

6. James Baldwin (1924-1987), U.S. writer
In a 1980 interview Baldwin said, "I spent my season in hell in the gay world, and there's nothing gay about it. I never understood that term. I don't trust any term. I love a few people; some are women, and some are men; and it is all much, much more complex than those obscure definitions allow."

7. Sir Peter Pears (1910-1986), British tenor
Pears was asked in a 1979 interview what he thought of the word *gay.* He said he hated it. "It gives quite a false impression," he remarked. "It's lovely when people are happy, but you just cannot call the whole homosexual movement gay." When pressed whether or not he would ever actively participate in the gay rights movement, he replied, "If confronted with a yes-or-no situation, I suppose I would take part in a gay liberation march or something, but it's not at all sympathetic to me."

22 Colorful Slang Expressions for Sodomy

1. Baking potatoes
2. Beef injection
3. Bending some ham
4. Packing fudge
5. Rump-splitting
6. Cornholing
7. Performing an embuggery
8. Fluting
9. Institutional cooking
10. Moon shot
11. Painting the bucket
12. Powdering the cheeks
13. Stirring the chocolate
14. Surfing
15. Oscaring
16. Mollying
17. Cowboying
18. Pigsticking
19. Making a windward passage
20. Queering
21. Dicking
22. Hot-dogging

16 Sex Practices and the Proper Technical Terms for Each

		Technical term
1.	Cock sucking	Penilingus, fellatio
2.	Dirty talk during sex	Coprolalia
3.	Rimming	Anilingus
4.	Licking the sweat off someone	Salirophilia
5.	Golden showers, water sports	Urolagnia
6.	Fucking in water (the shower, Jacuzzi, or swimming pool)	Undinism
7.	Fist fucking	Brachioproctis
8.	A three-way	Troilism
9.	A sexual interest in cigars	Capnolagnia

10. Sex with the dead . . . . Necrophilia
11. A sexual interest in children . . . . Pedophilia
12. Belly fucking, the Princeton Rub . . . . Frottage
13. A sexual preference for the elderly . . . Gerontophilia
14. A sexual interest in animals . . . . Zoophilia, bestiality
15. Mud wrestling, a sexual interest in filth . . . . Mysophilia
16. A sexual fascination with large dicks . . . . Phallophilia

7 Popular Positions for Jacking Off and the Advantages and Disadvantages of Each

1. Lying on back

Easily the most popular position, illustrated by Tom Cruise in the movie *Risky Business* and Dennis Christopher in *Fade to Black.* Advantages: Good angle for thrusting action with hips; keeps the sheets from getting messy; easy to keep dildo or butt plug in one's asshole; easy reach for either nipple. Disadvantages: Bad angle to look at pictures; monotonous when used day after day.

2. Standing up

Also very popular, especially with narcissists, men who cruise public bathrooms, and guys on the go. Advantages: You can watch yourself in the mirror; easy to do anywhere; convenient to do in the shower where the sound of running water masks the telltale noises you're making. Disadvantages: Knees and legs can get tired and buckle; come-splotched shoes, carpet, or floor; difficult to keep dildos in one's ass.

3. Legs thrown over head

In this position a guy lies on his back and throws his legs back over his head so that the head of his dick is aimed right at his mouth. Often used in S/M scenes as a way for the master to force his slave to eat his own come. Advantages: Intense orgasm; great if you're hungry for come, even your own; sexy position for watching yourself shoot off; leaves ass completely vulnerable. Disadvantages: Sprained neck and back; come can get in your eyes; difficult position to hold; bad angle for looking at dirty pictures.

4. On the belly, fucking fist

Advantages: Intense orgasm; most perfectly simulates actual intercourse; good angle for thrusting; good angle for looking at dirty pictures. Disadvantages: Messy sheets; awkward to do while being butt-fucked; difficult to reach nipples; parents, roommates, and lovers can sneak up on you without being detected.

5. On the belly, rubbing dick against sheets, pillows, etc.

Advantages: Good when you're in a lazy mood; good while being fucked up the ass; leaves both hands free to play with nipples or turn pages of magazine. Disadvantages: Messy sheets or wet pillow; come in pubic hair.

6. On one's knees

Advantages: Most convenient position while sucking cock or eating ass; enhances feelings of being dominated. Disadvantages: "Washer woman knees"; bad angle for thrusting with hips; come-splotched carpet or floor.

7. Sitting on toilet

Portnoy, among others, helped make this position famous, and it was immortalized in the movie *The Right Stuff.* Advantages: Good when you can't find any other way to be alone; towels are right there for clean-up; convenient when you're in a hurry. Disadvantage: Unappetizing location.

30 Picturesque Slang Expressions for Masturbation

1. Balling off
2. Bashing the bishop
3. Choking the chipmunk
4. Coming one's mutton
5. Cracking nuts
6. Dishonorable discharge
7. Dolloping the wiener
8. Fisting off
9. Flogging the poodle
10. Having one off the wrist
11. Jerking the gherkin
12. Manual labor
13. Paddling the pickle
14. Playing solitaire
15. Pocket pool
16. Pounding the pud
17. Pumping off
18. Punishing Percy in the palm
19. Singing an aria
20. Snapping the twig
21. Squeezing off
22. Stropping one's beak
23. Strumming the banjo
24. Taking care of business
25. Tap dancing
26. Tossing off
27. Wanking off
28. Waving the wand
29. Whacking off
30. Keeping a date with Rosie Palm and her five sisters

9 Animals, Other Than Humans, That Masturbate

1. Camels

Prodigious masturbators, male camels will often attempt to gratify themselves by pressing their penises down against the ground and rubbing themselves to orgasm. The same technique has also been observed among sheep.

2. Deer

Stags are known to masturbate several times a day and will even masturbate after having just experienced ejaculation with a female. The tips of their antlers are one of their most highly charged erogenous zones. The renowned English naturalist Frank Fraser Darling wrote of observing a stag who achieved instant erection simply by lowering his head and gently rubbing his antlers through some shrubbery. Spontaneous ejaculation followed within seconds.

3. Whales

Whales in captivity often masturbate by rubbing themselves against the bottoms of their pools or holding tanks. Males will also, on rare occasions, rub against one another.

4. Cats

Although tomcats are known to masturbate, they usually accomplish the act so discreetly—most often by gently licking their erections—that their human companions are completely unaware of what's going on. House cats will also sometimes masturbate by dragging a cloth between their hind legs and rubbing their genitals against it.

5. Porcupines

Male porcupines will frequently masturbate by rubbing their erections against sticks or other convenient protrusions in the wild.

6. Parrots

Parrots are especially prone to masturbate when bored in captivity and use a variety of methods, including gently nuzzling their penises with their beaks. They will also occasionally masturbate against convenient objects—blankets, sticks, toys—in their cages. In some instances they will masturbate against the hands of their human companions.

7. Elephants

For male elephants the preferred method of masturbation is to tuck the penis down between the hind legs and then rub the thighs together vigorously. The same technique has been observed in bears.

8. Dogs

Unneutered male dogs use a variety of methods to vent their sexual frustration when a mate isn't available. One of the simplest is autofellatio. More infamously, they may grab onto and begin humping the leg of a human companion, an activity known as "inappropriate mounting behavior."

9. Goats

Billy goats usually masturbate either through an act of autofellatio or by repeatedly stimulating the penis with one of their hoofs.

9 Victorian "Cures" for Masturbation

During the Victorian era, masturbation was the focus of extraordinary anxiety among doctors and parents; "curing" it became an obsession. The hysteria surrounding the subject was fueled by righteous moralists who regarded masturbation as a worse sin than adultery and by quack doctors who claimed that the loss of a single ounce of semen through masturbation was more debilitating to the body than the loss of several ounces of blood. One Victorian-era physician listed no fewer that 47 dire consequences of the act. Masturbation was believed to cause everything from acne and epilepsy to mental retardation and death. Hoping to eradicate this "scourge of young manhood," parents subjected their children to dozens of torturous cures.

1. Castration

Recalcitrant young masturbators were sometimes castrated to annihilate their sex urge. In some cases the entire penis was amputated, and voodooistic doctors used nightmarish reasoning to console the anguished parents: It was better to cut off a boy's genitals entirely than let him go insane or die from masturbating too much.

2. Straitjacket pajamas
Fearing that boys might masturbate in bed after the lights were turned out, some parents turned to pajama tops modeled after straitjackets. A boy's arms were laced into heavy sleeves that were then tied around the back of his body. Other parents gave new meaning to the admonishment "Keep your hands where I can see them" and simply tied their children's wrists to the bedposts every night.

3. Erection alarms
These were expensive and complicated devices. A flexible metal band was secured around the base of the penis and then attached, with wires, to a small box on the nightstand. When an erection occurred, the penis expanded and set off a loud electronic alarm. Parents sleeping in another room were notified that their son was on the verge of "abusing" himself—or of having a nocturnal emission, which was considered just as harmful.

4. Enemas
Some physicians preached that masturbation was caused by constipation or by a buildup of unhealthy germs in the bowels. They recommended that parents give their children daily morning enemas with ice water.

5. Infibulation
Some parents had their sons' foreskins fastened shut with rings, clasps, or staples to prevent erection and masturbation. In extreme cases the entire foreskin was sewn shut; only a tiny opening was left for urination.

6. Breakfast cereals
Many Victorian physicians believed that the key to preventing masturbation was good nutrition. With that in mind, they developed a variety of wholesome foods specifically designed to purge a child's body of unhealthy impulses. The American physician and health food pioneer John Harvey Kellogg introduced a new line of

such foods at his sanitarium in Battle Creek, Michigan. They were called Kellogg's Breakfast Cereals.

7. Die onaniebandagen

Literally "the masturbation bandage," this was developed in Germany and endorsed by noted sexologist Havelock Ellis. It consisted of a little metal suit of armor that fitted snugly over the penis and testicles and was attached to a lock. The parents, of course, kept the key.

8. Spiked cock rings

Cock rings with tiny razors or needle-like spikes on the inside were sometimes fitted around the base of a boy's penis to prevent him from attaining an erection.

9. Good, clean living

"There is only one way in which a boy can ever break the habit of self-abuse," claimed the nineteenth-century sex guide *Light on Dark Corners.* "He must determine to do it and he must be dead-in-earnest about it. The one supreme factor in the fight is a determined will. A boy can control his morbid curiosity about sex subjects if he will think on other matters. He can drive out the memory of old base pictures and stories and suggestions if he will simply determine to set his mind on the subjects that are fine and clean. And remember, there is no greater single means of help in the fight than to try definitely to help someone else in the same battle. It is wonderful how we get new strength when we try to help a friend break a bad habit that may also be afflicting us. So, pitch in and give a lift to the other fellow, for your own sake as well as for his."

10 Substances Often Reputed to Be Aphrodisiacs

1. Strychnine
Strychnine's rather unlikely reputation as an aphrodisiac is based on its effect on the central nervous system: Ingesting a very small amount is said to heighten sensitivity to all stimulation. However, it is an extremely toxic poison. Less than five milligrams will kill a person, and death is usually the result of physical exhaustion after a series of excruciating convulsions. The line between a stimulating dose and a lethal one is so fine that taking it, even under the pretense of trying to increase one's sexual pleasure, is more a suicidal act than a hedonistic one.

2. Chocolate
Noted sexologist Havelock Ellis believed that chocolate was an aphrodisiac. Unfortunately, there is no evidence to support his belief. Chocolate is rich in carbohydrates—as well as protein, phosphorus, and calcium—and is therefore an excellent source of quick energy. It also contains minute amounts of caffeine and theobromine, a diuretic. Its reputation as an aphrodisiac was once so strong that seventeenth-century monks were forbidden to eat it lest their minds become filled with lewd thoughts and fantasies.

3. Ginseng
Ginseng has been used as an aphrodisiac by the Chinese for thousands of years and has recently gained wide popularity in the U.S. *Panax quinquefolius* is the North American variety, grown mostly in the Appalachian mountain region, but its aphrodisiac effects are said to be considerably less than those of its Oriental cousin, *Panax schinseng.* Most often made as a stimulating tea, ginseng is also said to soothe the nerves, prolong youth, and help the body fight off infection.

4. L-dopa

The powerful drug L-dopa—levodihydroxyphenylalanine—was first used in the late 1960s to treat people suffering from Parkinson's disease. Today, it is also used, surreptitiously, by some athletes to increase the effectiveness of steroids and pituitary growth hormone. Hypersexuality is a side effect reported in some users. Other side effects, however, include heart disease, skin tumors, and various neurological disorders.

5. Spanish fly

Perhaps the most commonly known of all alleged aphrodisiacs, Spanish fly is a delicate powder, the desiccated remains of a southern European beetle, *Cantharis vesicatoria.* The Marquis de Sade was infamous for serving guests little chocolate bonbons filled with Spanish fly—a practice that eventually led to his arrest after several prostitutes were poisoned by them. Its alleged aphrodisiac power is an accidental result of its action on the genitourinary tract: It causes acute irritation of the mucous membrane of the urethra and a dilation of associated blood vessels around the genitals. However, it does not, in itself, increase sexual desire. Instead, it usually causes severe inflammation, violent illness, convulsions, or death.

6. Honey

Honey figures prominently in various Arabic sex manuals, including *The Perfumed Garden* and the *Kama Sutra.* To increase sexual prowess, *The Perfumed Garden* recommended drinking a glassful of honey and eating twenty almonds every night, for three nights, before going to bed. To heighten orgasm, it recommended drinking honey spiced with nutmeg. The ancient Greeks also valued honey as an aphrodisiac; honey-sesame cakes baked in the shape of genitals were said to have aphrodisiac powers. Honey is rich in B vitamins, amino acids, and enzymes. It is also one of the most easily digested foods known.

7. Prairie oysters

Regarded as a delicacy by some (and as a gastronomic atrocity by others), prairie oysters are bull testicles and are a popular item in some restaurants in the Rocky Mountain region, where they are also known as "Rocky Mountain oysters." For the full aphrodisiac effect, they are supposed to be eaten raw and as fresh as possible. Although they contain some male sex hormones, most of these hormones are apparently destroyed in the stomach during digestion. The ancient Chinese and Hindus believed that tiger testicles were also an aphrodisiac. And among some cannibalistic peoples, raw human genitals were ingested for their supposed ability to increase sexual desire and prowess.

8. Sarsaparilla

In the sixteenth century sarsaparilla was used, unsuccessfully, in the treatment of syphilis and rheumatism. In the nineteenth century it was regarded as a blood purifier and as a cure for general lethargy and weakness. Its reputation as an aphrodisiac goes back several centuries to Mexico and Latin and South America, where various parts of the aromatic herb are still used to make invigorating teas and tonics. In the 1940s a Hungarian scientist living in Mexico, Dr. Emerick Solmo, claimed to have discovered that the root of the plant contains a chemical similar in structure to testosterone, a primary male sex hormone in humans. His findings were subject to much dispute and derision. Sarsaparilla's primary use in the U.S. has been as a flavoring in soft drinks.

9. Vitamin E

Vitamin E has been hailed as a cure for everything from varicose veins and senility to cancer and old age. A vitamin E deficiency can apparently cause sterility and impotence in men, but whether megadoses of it can improve one's sex life is unknown. Several forms of vitamin E exist in nature, but alpha tocopherol, the most powerful form, is of greatest importance nutritionally. Some of the richest sources of vitamin E are wheat germ, scallops, peanuts, margarine, safflower oil, and raw leeks.

10. Yohimbine

A crystalline substance, alkaloid in nature, yohimbine was once one of the most widely prescribed drugs for increasing the sex drive. It is derived from the bark of a tree native to central Africa, where it has long been used by the natives to increase sexual desire and improve sexual performance. Its primary medical use in the U.S. has been in the treatment of neuritis and meningitis. Because it stimulates the lower spinal nerves controlling erection, it has acquired a reputation as an aphrodisiac and has sometimes been used in the treatment of impotence and sexual apathy.

12 Substances Reputed to Diminish Sexual Desire and Performance

1. Aspirin
2. Cocaine
3. Digitalis
4. Sodium bicarbonate
5. Menthol
6. Potassium nitrate (saltpeter)
7. Hard liquor
8. Tobacco
9. Quinine
10. Lemon juice
11. Lime juice
12. Vinegar

12 Famous People Who Believed in the Power of Aphrodisiacs

1. Aristotle (384-322 B.C.), **Greek philosopher**
Recommended the use of oil of peppermint to stimulate sexual desire. To reduce the libido, he suggested walking long distances through the hills barefoot.

2. Pliny (A.D. 23-79), Roman naturalist
To fan the flames of lust, he suggested eating a hyena eye with a dash of licorice or dill.

3. Niccolo Machiavelli (1469-1527), Italian statesman and writer
Often praised the aphrodisiac powers of the mandrake plant and wrote a ribald comedy, *Mandragola,* in its honor.

4. Francois Rabelais (1490-1553), French writer
Recommended marzipan, or claret spiced with cinnamon.

5. Giovanni Giacomo Casanova (1725-1798), Italian libertine and adventurer
Attributed much of his spectacular sexual energy to the fact that he downed 50 oysters for breakfast every morning.

6. Captain James Cook (1728-1779), English explorer
The first European ever to set foot on the Hawaiian Islands, Cook feasted every morning on a special aphrodisiac dish composed of fresh shrimp. He often boasted that he could take on ten native girls a day.

7. Madame Dubarry (1743-1793), mistress of Louis XV
She tried to keep Louis XV in her power by feeding him foods that would make him weak with lust: sweetbreads, venison, pheasant cooked in white wine, truffles, capon in sherry broth, to name just a few. "She makes me forget that soon I will be sixty," Louis told a friend.

8. Sir Richard Burton (1821-1890), English explorer and writer
Was especially convinced of the aphrodisiac powers of hashish and published recipes for making it correctly.

9. Havelock Ellis (1859-1939), English sexologist
Praised the aphrodisiac powers of alcohol (in small doses), beefsteak, and chocolate. Also believed that perfumes were a powerful aphrodisiac.

10. **Mae West (1892-1980), U.S. actress**
The legendary sex queen recommended eating almonds to increase one's sex drive and improve one's sex life.

11. **Duke Ellington (1899-1974), U.S. jazz musician**
Touted both vodka and caviar as aphrodisiacs.

12. **Timothy Leary (b. 1922), U.S. psychologist and LSD advocate**
Once claimed that "LSD is the most powerful aphrodisiac ever discovered by man."

Ages When 14 Famous Men First Had Sex With Another Man

1. **Edward Albee (b. 1928), U.S. playwright**
The Pulitzer prize-winning playwright first began having sex when he was twelve or thirteen. "I went away to boys' schools—Lawrenceville, Valley Forge Military Academy, and Choate—and we were fucking all the time," he told an interviewer. He took to homosexuality, he said, "like a duck to water."

2. **Greg Louganis (b. 1960), U.S. diver**
Louganis engaged in typical sexual experimentation with other boys during adolescence but didn't actually have sex until he was sixteen. His partner was an older man he met at the beach one afternoon after school. "On the drive home I could smell his scent on me," Louganis recalled in his autobiography, *Breaking the Surface.* "I was worried that my mother would know I had been with a man. As soon as I got home, I jumped in the shower and scrubbed myself clean." Louganis saw the man several more times after that. "I hated the separateness and the secrecy," he noted, "but I kept going back for the affection.... I was starved for affection."

3. **W. Somerset Maugham (1874-1965), British writer**
Maugham was sixteen and studying in Heidelberg, Germany, when he first had sex with another man, a 26-year-old British student he met there.

4. **Robert Mapplethorpe (1946-1989), U.S. photographer**
When Mapplethorpe was sixteen, he masturbated over the steamier passages in *Lady Chatterley's Lover* as well as over nudist magazines his parents kept hidden in their bedroom closet. He also stole a gay porn magazine from a store on 42nd Street in New York City. But he resisted identifying himself as homosexual. It wasn't until he was in his early twenties and had had a tumultuous heterosexual relationship with poet and rock star Patti Smith that he began having sex with men, during a college vacation to San Francisco. "It was like it happened overnight," Smith later recalled of Mapplethorpe's seemingly abrupt embrace of a gay identity. "The gay thing wasn't there, and then suddenly it was."

5. **RuPaul (b. 1957), U.S. drag artist and entertainer**
He first had sex with another man the day after his eighteenth birthday. His partner was a thirty-six-year-old counselor who found him attractive but wouldn't have sex with him until he was of legal age. "The day after [I turned eighteen] I went to his house," RuPaul later recalled. RuPaul remembered the experience as "very wonderful."

6. **Oscar Wilde (1854-1900), British playwright and wit**
Wilde was thirty-two—and had already been married for two years—before he actually had sex with another man. His partner was a college student, Robert Ross, who became one of Wilde's lifelong friends and his literary executor.

7. **Michelangelo Signorile (b. 1958), U.S. writer**
The self-styled maven of outing first had sex with another man when he was twelve years old. "My...hormones were beginning to rage," he wrote in his book *Queer in America.* "I was an early developer, with hair on my chest...." His partner was a thirty-year-old

man whom Signorile purposefully sought out. "Certainly I, as an adult," he wrote, "would never have sex with a twelve-year-old and would consider anyone, straight or gay, who did so as behaving irresponsibly. But if it hadn't been him, it would have been someone else...." The encounter, though physically enjoyable, left him wracked with guilt for days.

8. Christopher Isherwood (1904-1986), English-U.S. writer
He realized he was gay when he was ten and often had orgasms wrestling with other boys. He was also sexually attracted to his father. "I used to go into his dressing room in the morning while he was doing physical exercises almost naked, in his undershorts," he once said. "I can still remember liking the hardness of his muscles and the smell of his body." But it wasn't until Isherwood was in college, in his late teens or early twenties, that he actually had sex with another man.

9. Scott Thompson (b. 1958), Canadian comedian
Best known as the gay member of the popular comedy troupe The Kids in the Hall, Thompson had his first sexual experience with another man when he was barely in his twenties and attending York University in Toronto as a theater arts major. "I was seeing a girl at the time," he later recalled, "but I got picked up by this campus football player, and he took me into a stairwell, and we did it there.... I couldn't believe what I'd done, and I was catatonic for days. It took me three years before I did it again." Having thought of himself as bisexual for years, he finally acknowledged his homosexuality to himself when he was twenty-four.

10. Tennessee Williams (1912-1983), U.S. playwright
Although he'd had wet dreams and spontaneous orgasms, he didn't even masturbate until he was twenty-seven, and it wasn't until he was twenty-eight that he first had sex with another man—a paratrooper in New Orleans.

11. E.M. Forster (1879-1970), English writer
Forster spent his teens and twenties in a state of unrelieved sexual

frustration. Finally, when he was thirty-one, a longtime friend made love to him on a sitting-room sofa; it was the first time Forster had had any kind of physical encounter with another man. "After so long a delay," biographer P.N. Furbank wrote, "the event was not, after all, of much significance to Forster."

12. **John Addington Symonds (1840-1893), English essayist and historian**
Symonds anguished over his homosexual impulses for years and suffered from one physical malady after another as he tried to suppress them. At the age of thirty-six, he finally hired "a brawny young soldier" to have sex with him at a male brothel in London. The experience, Symonds wrote, "exercised a powerful effect upon my life." It did not cure his physical maladies—in fact, he suffered a severe relapse of lung disease shortly afterward—but it set him on the road to coming to grips with his real nature.

13. **Dave Pallone (b. 1952), U.S. umpire**
Pallone was twenty-six and umpiring winter baseball in Puerto Rico when he met a "strikingly handsome" young Puerto Rican by the beach. Pallone, who had previously engaged only in homosexual experimentation during his teen years, invited the young man up to his condominium for a beer. After some initial uncertainty and shyness on both men's parts, the two had sex. "The next hour was pure sexual passion," Pallone later recalled. "What did it feel like? The same as heterosexual passion: breathlessness, dizziness, heat. I lost my inhibitions and almost my consciousness, and I became what my body felt. And something else: I knew instinctively that while I was doing this, I was the person I had always imagined myself to be." Although Pallone had suspected he was gay since adolescence, he had allowed himself to have sex only with women up to that time.

14. **David Kopay (b. 1942), U.S. football pro**
He was twenty or twenty-one when he first had sex with another man. His partner was a fraternity brother at the University of Washington. The two of them had been out one night drinking

beer. When they came home, they collapsed in bed together. "We kept our clothes on," Kopay later wrote, "but I had an orgasm just from rubbing against Ted and holding him." He and Ted repeated the experience numerous times together while they were in college, eventually advancing to intercourse and oral sex.

14 Men Who Paid at Least Once for Gay Sex

1. Barney Frank (b. 1940), U.S. congressman
2. Roy Cohn (1927-1986), U.S. attorney
3. Paul Lynde (1926-1982), U.S. entertainer
4. Pier Paolo Pasolini (1922-1975), Italian film director
5. Cecil Beaton (1904-1980), English photographer and designer
6. George Cukor (1899-1983), U.S. film director
7. Charles Laughton (1899-1962), English actor
8. Cole Porter (1893-1964), U.S. songwriter
9. T.E. Lawrence (1888-1935), English adventurer and writer
10. Monty Woolley (1888-1963), U.S. actor
11. W. Somerset Maugham (1874-1965), English writer
12. A.E. Housman (1859-1936), English poet
13. Sir Richard Burton (1821-1890), English explorer and writer
14. Sophocles (496-406 B.C.), Greek tragic poet

13 Men Who Have Been Paid at Least Once for Their Sexual Services

1. RuPaul (b. 1957), U.S. drag artist and entertainer
2. Michael Kearns (b. 1951), U.S. actor
3. Robert Mapplethorpe (1946-1989), U.S. photographer
4. John Preston (1945-1994), U.S. writer
5. Casey Donovan (1943-1987), U.S. porn star
6. John Rechy (b. 1934), U.S. writer
7. Jean Genet (1910-1986), French writer
8. Alexander Menshikov (1672-1729), Russian general and confidant to Peter the Great
9. Elagabalus (205-222), Roman emperor
10. Domitian (51-96), Roman emperor
11. Octavius (63 B.C.-A.D. 14), Roman emperor
12. Agathocles (361-289 B.C.), tyrant of Syracuse
13. Phaedo of Elis (418 B.C.-?), disciple of Socrates

16 Famous Men, All Reputedly Very Well-Hung

1. Jason Priestley (b. 1969), Canadian actor
Film editors working on his 1993 movie *Calendar Girl* reportedly had to use computers to touch up the footage from the film's skinny-dipping sequence: Priestley's endowment was so large, it kept showing, no matter what camera angle had been used. Producers wanted a PG-13 rating, not the inevitable R they would have gotten had any part of Priestley's penis been visible.

2. Lord Byron (1788-1824), English poet
His reputation as a libertine prevented him from being buried in Poets' Corner at Westminster Abbey, and he was interred instead in a small church near Nottingham, England. In 1938, 114 years after his death, the burial vault was opened, and Byron's body was found to be well-preserved with the features easily recognizable. One observer noted: "His sexual organ shewed quite abnormal development."

3. Errol Flynn (1909-1959), U.S. actor
He was obsessively proud of the size of his penis and, according to Truman Capote, took it out of his pants at a party one night and tried to play "You Are My Sunshine" on the piano with it.

4. James Woods (b. 1947), U.S. actor
His extraordinarily large endowment was, for years, the subject of numerous ribald jokes in Hollywood during the 1980s. Woods's former girlfriend Sean Young once told a reporter, "God would have been merciful if he had given him a little teeny penis so that he could get on with his life."

5. Frank Sinatra (b. 1915) U.S. singer
When his second wife, actress Ava Gardner, was asked what she saw in the "one-hundred-twenty-pound runt," she replied, "Well, there's only ten pounds of Frank, but there's one hundred and ten pounds of cock!"

6. Arnold Schwarzenegger (b. 1947), Austrian-U.S. actor and bodybuilder
Schwarzenegger had the distinction of being named to *Gentlemen's Quarterly*'s 1990 list of twenty-three of the best-hung men in modern history. Among the list's other honorees: Warren Beatty, Matt Dillon, Marlon Brando, Nicky Hilton, Humphrey Bogart, Robert Redford, John Derek, Babe Ruth, and John F. Kennedy.

7. Aristotle Onassis (1906-1975), Greek shipping magnate

He sometimes referred to his huge penis as "the secret of my success" and once dragged an obnoxious reporter into a men's room to prove just how well-hung he was. Maria Callas told a friend, "When I met Aristo, so full of life, I became a different woman."

8. Milton Berle (b. 1908), U.S. entertainer
Berle's reputation for being well-hung was so well-known that he was challenged to a bet by a stranger who claimed his penis was bigger than Berle's. Berle took the man into a nearby rest room to settle the wager; but despite goading from his friends to show off the whole thing, Berle would pull out only enough to win the bet.

9. Charlie Chaplin (1889-1977), U.S. filmmaker and actor
He cheerfully referred to himself as "the Eighth Wonder of the World."

10. Fatty Arbuckle (1887-1933), U.S. silent-screen comedian
In 1921, after a three-day wild party that left the twelfth floor of San Francisco's Hotel St. Francis in shambles, the 300-pound comedian was charged with manslaughter in the death of a young starlet he had allegedly raped. The girl had died of peritonitis and a ruptured bladder, leading to rumors about Arbuckle's supposedly gargantuan endowment. After two mistrials Arbuckle was finally acquitted of the murder, but by then Paramount had canceled his contract, and his career was finished.

11. Charles II (1630-1685), king of England
He was nicknamed "Old Rowley" after a studhorse he owned. It was sometimes joked that his scepter and his penis were of equal length.

12. Gary Cooper (1901-1961), U.S. actor
Cooper's reputation for being exceptionally well-hung helped accelerate his notoriety as one of Hollywood's most prodigious lovers. When Tallulah Bankhead was asked why she was leaving New York for Hollywood in the 1940s, she said it was "to fuck that divine Gary Cooper."

13. John Dillinger (1902-1934), U.S. bank robber
For years it was rumored that his penis was an incredible 14 inch-

es long when flaccid, 20 to 22 inches long when erect. However, one eyewitness to Dillinger's autopsy later testified that the outlaw had a normal endowment.

14. Jack London (1876-1916), U.S. writer
The handsome, muscular writer was often referred to as "the Stallion" by his friends.

15. Aldo Ray (1926-1991), U.S. actor
After making a name for himself as a character actor in such films as *Miss Sadie Thompson* and *God's Little Acre,* his Hollywood career started to slide in the early '60s. He then jumped into the burgeoning porno movie business, where his husky good looks and extra-large endowment helped him find a whole new audience of admirers.

16. Henri de Toulouse-Lautrec (1864-1901), French artist
Crippled in adolescence, he never grew taller than 5 foot 1, but his genitals were unusually large, even for a man of normal size. Referring to his squat body and enormous cock, he described himself as "a coffeepot with a big spout." Friends sometimes referred to him as *verges a pattes*: "a walking penis."

Hung Like a Horse: Average Erect Penis Lengths for 10 Species

Average Erect Penis Length

1. Humpback whale . . . . 10 ft.
2. Elephant . . . . 5 to 6 ft.
3. Bull . . . . 3 ft.
4. Stallion . . . . 2 ft. 6 in.
5. Rhinoceros . . . . 2 ft.

6. Pig .... 18 to 20 in.
7. Man .... 6 in.
8. Gorilla .... 2 in.
9. Cat .... ¾ in.
10. Mosquito .... 1/100 in.

6 Renowned Male Nudes

1. Praxiteles' *Eros* (4th century B.C.)
Praxiteles' sculpture portrayed Eros, the young god of passion, as a virile and beautiful nude teenage boy. The sculpture—a gift to the ancient Greek town of Thespiae—was so lifelike and seductive that one visitor, Allketas the Rhodian, fell in love with it and masturbated against it frequently, leaving, according to the historian Pliny, the "traces of his lust" all over it. Later the emperor Nero became so enamored of it that he had it brought back to Rome; it perished there in the great fire of A.D. 64.

2. Michelangelo's *David* (1504)
Michelangelo was only twenty-nine when he completed his *David.* The eighteen-foot-high sculpture, carved from a damaged slab of Carrara marble, was quickly dubbed *Il gigante,* "The Giant." After the statue was erected on the porch of the Palazzo Vecchio, scandalized Florentines initially stoned it overnight, and in the nearly five centuries since, it has at various times been fitted with a fig leaf. In 1975 British novelist Anthony Burgess shuddered at the sculpture's unabashed homoeroticism. "It invokes unpleasing visions of Michelangelo slavering over male beauty," he complained. Michelangelo was paid only about $5,000 for the thirty months he labored over the sculpture.

3. Caravaggio's *Victorious Amor* (1600)
Caravaggio's seventeenth-century paintings have been called "nude pin-ups masquerading as religious works," and during his lifetime

Caravaggio was often condemned for the blatantly homoerotic naturalism of his work; some of his contemporaries were outraged at his use of Roman street hustlers and other young gamins as models for revered religious figures in devotional paintings. However, his paintings were otherwise extremely popular, especially with one of his patrons, Cardinal Francesco del Monte, a highly influential papal prelate who was also a renowned pedophiliac. *Victorious Amor* remains the quintessential Caravaggio work, with Cupid erotically portrayed as a naked, seductive, prepubescent boy gleefully trouncing various symbols of human achievement and sophistication. Art critic Michael Jacobs has noted, "The great popularity of a painting like the *Victorious Amor*...is proof of how large the market in child pornography was, and how successfully Caravaggio had cornered it."

4. Statue of St. Guignole (18th century)

In northwest France a nude marble statue of St. Guignole achieved fame in the 1700s for its alleged powers to cure infertility and frigidity. Desperate women took scrapings from the statue's large penis, mixed the scrapings with water, and then drank the mixture. This created a problem for the shrine's monks, who were kept busy constantly repairing or replacing the statue's genitals. Their final solution was ingenious: They drilled a large hole through the statue's groin and inserted a long penis made of wood down through it. As fanatical devotees scraped the penis down in size, a blow with a mallet from the rear would suddenly cause the saint's organ to regain its original length.

5. Aubrey Beardsley's *Examination of the Herald* (1896)

Drawn when Aubrey Beardsley was twenty-three, *The Examination of the Herald* was part of a series of illustrations for an expensive, private edition of Aristophanes's ribald comedy *Lysistrata. The Examination* shows a beautiful young messenger boy with a huge erect penis as thick as his thighs and several feet long. The work, along with several of Beardsley's other illustrations for the book, was denounced by many of his contemporaries as shockingly lewd. Oscar Wilde, on the other hand, thought that Beardsley had "brought a strangely new personality to English art.... Absinthe is to all other drinks what Aubrey's drawings are to other pictures." In the year before his death, Beardsley converted to Roman Catholicism and recanted all of his erotic drawings. "I implore you to destroy all copies of *Lysistrata,*" he wrote his publisher. Happily, his wishes were not obeyed. Beardsley was only twenty-five when he died. In its obituary for him, *The New York Times* dismissed his work "as a passing fad" and confidently predicted: "A coming age will wonder why there was any brief interest taken in Beardsley's work."

6. Centerfold of Burt Reynolds (1972)
Riding high on a growing wave of sexual liberation for women, *Cosmopolitan* magazine published the first mainstream nude centerfold of a man in April 1972: a photograph of "macho" movie star Burt Reynolds, then thirty-six, naked (except for his genitals coyly covered) on a tiger skin rug. Reynolds's picture cleared the way for "beefcake" magazines for women, notably *Playgirl* and *Viva.* The issue with Reynolds's centerfold was touted as the largest-selling issue of any magazine in publishing history. Across the ocean, the English edition of *Cosmopolitan* also featured a nude centerfold that month: not of Burt Reynolds, but of feminist Germaine Greer's husband, construction worker Paul de Feu. De Feu described his posing as "striking a blow for male servitude."

3 Fascinating Severed Penises

1. Rasputin's penis
When Grigori Rasputin, the mad monk of Russia, was finally murdered in 1916 by a conspiracy of Russian aristocrats—led by the bisexual royalist Prince Felix Yussoupov—his penis and testicles were allegedly hacked off with a hunting knife by the assassins and

then flung disparagingly across the room. The act was meant as a final, befitting indignity for a man whose sexual rapacity was legendary, so legendary that stories of Rasputin's sex life (and rumors he had been sleeping with the Empress Alexandra) helped bring down Tsar Nicholas II and the Russian monarchy. The severed organ—reputed to be thirteen inches long when erect—was quickly seized by a servant. According to various sources, the amputated penis was then passed on to one of Rasputin's former lovers, who faithfully preserved it in a long wooden box by her bedside in Paris. An observer who claimed to have once glimpsed the relic described it as having the appearance of an "overripe banana."

2. Napoleon's penis

Napoleon's penis was removed by one of his doctors during an autopsy following the former emperor's death in 1821. At that time it was noted that the organ was "small and apparently atrophied. He is said to have been impotent for some time before he died." One hundred and fifty years later, the penis turned up for sale, with several of Napoleon's belongings, at Christie's auction house in London. (Nervous at giving offense to its patrons, Christie's described the detached organ as "a small dried-up object.") The penis failed to attain the necessary bid but was finally sold several years later for nearly $4,000 to an American urologist.

3. John Wayne Bobbitt's penis

On June 23, 1993, Virginia manicurist Lorena Bobbitt achieved national celebrity when she used an eight-inch kitchen knife to slice off her husband's penis: She claimed he had come home drunk that night and raped her. With the bloody organ in hand, she jumped in the family car and drove off to a friend's house. She eventually tossed the severed penis out the car window. A few minutes later, however, she stopped at a nearby pay phone and called police to tell them where it was. The organ, eventually recovered by a volunteer fireman, was rushed to the hospital for reattachment to Lorena's husband, John Wayne Bobbitt, a 26-year-old ex-Marine. The reattachment surgery—which lasted over nine hours and cost over $50,000—was a success, and the Bobbitts became overnight celebrities and the subject of radio and television talk shows, magazine articles, and stand-up comedy routines. (One Los Angeles radio station sponsored the Lorena Bobbitt Weenie Toss: Women were invited to toss hot dogs at a target in order to win a free night out on the town.) Lorena, who accused her husband of a pattern of abuse throughout their marriage, was later acquitted of all charges in the case. John Wayne Bobbitt went on to parlay his notoriety into a million-dollar film deal: He starred in a hard-core porn video, *John Wayne Bobbitt Uncut.* The film—which featured numerous close-ups of the famous organ, both limp and erect—was described by *Entertainment Weekly* as "a freak show… bad…and yet it attains a gross fascination."

15 Famous Uncircumcised Men

1. Boy George
2. Marlon Brando
3. Johnny Carson
4. Tony Danza
5. Fabio
6. William Hurt
7. Billy Idol
8. Jesse Jackson
9. Magic Johnson
10. Eddie Murphy
11. Nick Nolte
12. Ronald Reagan
13. Arnold Schwarzenegger
14. Tom Selleck
15. Frank Sinatra

15 Famous Circumcised Men

1. Warren Beatty
2. Tom Cruise
3. Matt Dillon
4. Phil Donahue
5. Clint Eastwood
6. Doug Flutie
7. Mel Gibson
8. Wayne Groetsky
9. Mick Jagger
10. David Letterman
11. Oliver North
12. Donny Osmond
13. Sean Penn
14. Richard Simmons
15. Gore Vidal

15 Eighteenth-Century Slang Expressions for "Cock"

1. Creamstick
2. Dirk
3. Flute
4. Jock
5. Leather stretcher
6. Lobcock
7. Peacemaker
8. Pikestaff
9. Pilgrim's staff
10. Plug-tail
11. Plum-tree shaker
12. Pump handle
13. Rump-splitter
14. Star-gazer
15. Sugarstick

20 Nineteenth-Century Slang Expressions for "Cock"

1. Baby-maker
2. Bushwhacker
3. Cranny hunter
4. Dingle-dangle
5. Gravy giver
6. His Majesty in purple cap
7. Jiggling bone
8. John Thomas
9. Little brother
10. Lollipop
11. Man-root
12. Nature's scythe
13. Old slimy
14. Pile-driver
15. Pistol
16. Rammer
17. Trouser snake
18. Waterworks
19. Winkle
20. Yum-yum

12 Words or Phrases That Sound Obscene But Aren't

1. Tonguer
One who makes or inserts the tongues of shoes.

2. Cuntlines
The indented spiral intervals formed between the strands of a rope.

3. Mouthbreeder
Any of several varieties of fish that hatch and care for their young in the mouth.

4. Bunghole
The hole in a cask, through which it is emptied or filled.

5. Cockhead
The top of a grinding-mill spindle.

6. Titman
The runt in a litter of pigs.

7. Cummingtonite
A type of mineral composed of magnesium-iron silicate.

8. Prick shooting
Shooting with bow and arrow at a fixed mark.

9. Buttstrap
In carpentry, a strap or plate covering a butt joint.

10. Dick-ass
A donkey.

11. Cockmaster
A trainer or breeder of game cocks.

12. Armpit sniffer
A person employed to test the effectiveness of deodorants by sniffing the armpits of test subjects.

The Origins of 7 Common Sex-Related Words

1. Testicles
In ancient Rome the word *testari* meant "to be a witness." A derivative of the word—*testes*—came to refer to a man's testicles, since these were a witness to his manhood. *Testimony, testament,* and *testify* were all derived from the same root as *testicles.*

2. Penis
Penis shares the same origin as the words *pencil* and *penicillin.* All are derived from the Latin *penis,* which meant "a tail."

3. Cock
As a synonym for *penis,* the word *cock* dates back at least to the sixteenth century. It was likely derived from an earlier and still current use of the word to mean "a spout or short pipe through which liquid passes." In a sexual context it was not considered lewd or impolite until the early 1800s. It can be found in Shakespeare's *Henry V* (1599): "Pistol's cock is up, and flashing fire will follow." Laurence Olivier's 1945 film version of the play retained the line, but the censors of the day were either too ignorant or, less probably, too enlightened to object to it.

4. Semen
Semen is derived from the Latin *semen,* meaning "seed." The word *seminary*—"a place where intellectual seeds are sown"—also came from *semen.*

5. Dick
Dick probably came from the older English word *dirk,* meaning "a small sword." *Dirk,* in turn, was derived from *dorke,* meaning "the horns of an animal." *Dirk* and *dork* were also once slang expressions for "penis."

6. Come, cum
The origin of *come* for "semen" is not exactly known. As a verb, *come* has had a sexual sense at least since the sixteenth century, when the phrases *come at* and *come in unto* referred to sexual intercourse. In the nineteenth century, *come,* again as a verb, referred to the highly suggestive context of butter forming in a churn: The butter had *come*; that is, it had formed. Another possible connection is the seventeenth-century English word *coome,* which referred to a kind of very sweet honey. The alternate spelling *cum* probably originated with writers and editors who wanted an easy way for the eye to distinguish it from the more common verb *to come.*

7. Masturbate

There are two theories of where the word *masturbate* comes from. One holds that it is derived from the Latin words *mazdo,* meaning "penis," and *turba,* meaning "agitation": agitation of the penis. Another claims that it is from the Latin words *manus,* meaning "hand," and *stuprare,* meaning "defilement": to defile oneself with one's hand.

15 Provocatively Named Businesses

1. B&D Supermarket (South Carolina)
2. Leatherman's Feed & Seed (Memphis, Tennessee)
3. Gay Drugs (Redford, Michigan)
4. Younger Cock Tavern (London, England)
5. Dick's Drilling (Amarillo, Texas)
6. The Master Baiter (Isleton, California)
7. Salty Seaman Tavern (Columbus, Ohio)
8. Queen City Tire (Allentown, Penn.)
9. S&M Fixtures and Cabinets (Minneapolis)
10. S&M Motorcycle Repair (Edmonton, Alberta)
11. Bun Boy Motel (Southern California)
12. Rim Cafe (Heber, Arizona)
13. Kum-N-Go Market (Glendale, Arizona)
14. Dykeland Center (Sterling Heights, Michigan)
15. Golden Spread Pumping Service (Amarillo, Texas)

Scott O'Hara's Top 10 Travel Destinations for Gay Sex

Former gay porn star Scott O'Hara is an accomplished publisher, editor, and writer. As well as publishing *Wilde* magazine, he is the editor of *Steam,* a quarterly journal devoted to "sex and controversy." *Steam* was started when a friend jokingly suggested to O'Hara, "You should start a journal about your sex travels." It has since evolved into a magazine that mixes gritty first-person accounts of sometimes controversial sex practices with insightful dialogue on censorship and issues of sexual freedom: "a declaration," as O'Hara puts it, "that sex is not bad."

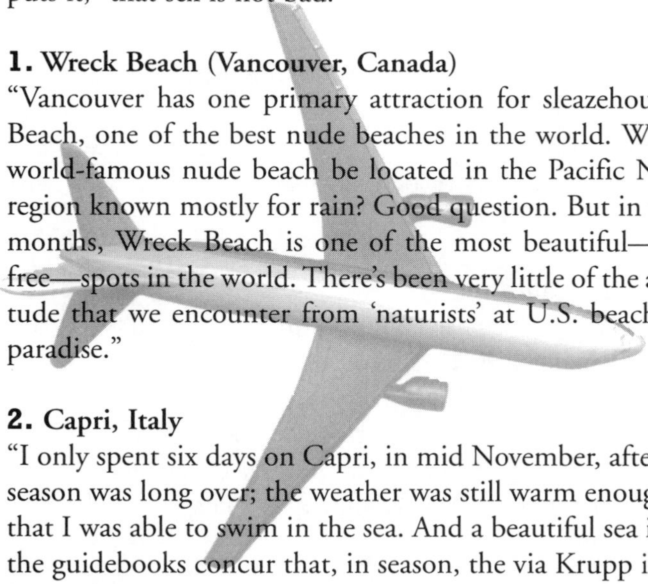

1. Wreck Beach (Vancouver, Canada)
"Vancouver has one primary attraction for sleazehounds: Wreck Beach, one of the best nude beaches in the world. Why should a world-famous nude beach be located in the Pacific Northwest, a region known mostly for rain? Good question. But in the summer months, Wreck Beach is one of the most beautiful—and hassle-free—spots in the world. There's been very little of the anti-sex attitude that we encounter from 'naturists' at U.S. beaches. And it's paradise."

2. Capri, Italy
"I only spent six days on Capri, in mid November, after the tourist season was long over; the weather was still warm enough, however, that I was able to swim in the sea. And a beautiful sea it is, too! All the guidebooks concur that, in season, the via Krupp is a smorgasbord of willing male flesh, and the beach below is a veritable outdoor orgy. In November there were very few men there; but the two that I most wanted proved to be available. (I saw one of them later with his girlfriend/wife. He grinned at me. European men are so civilized.) Take a sturdy, well-broken-in pair of hiking boots with you, as 90% of the joy of Capri, for me, was walking over the

entire island, peak to peak. I could've spent a month there, if the rains hadn't arrived."

3. Honolulu, Hawaii

"During the eighteen months I lived here, I think I had more sex than in the twelve years since then. Of course, this was due in part to the fact that I wasn't doing anything else; going to the beach and finding someone to fuck were the two most important things on my morning agenda. And, of course, I was working at the baths. The climate contributes to a laziness, a loss of time-sense, that approximates the situations in most bathhouses. I was living in a one-room apartment two blocks from the beach in Waikiki, and I loved running down to the beach in just my ratty old shorts for a midnight swim, often when high. I also discovered that if I Nair-ed my entire body, and then oiled myself up with baby oil, I could slip through the water like an eel, and every separate nerve ending in my entire body seemed to feel the water caressing me like a lover—a nearly orgasmic experience. On the whole, I prefer being in a work-oriented place, like Wisconsin or even San Francisco; but when you're in need of a place devoted to physical sensation, I recommend Hawaii."

4. Russian River, California

"The Wohler Bridge Beach is about as rural as you can get (but cruisy), and even downtown Guerneville still looks more like a small town than a resort. I can't recommend a visit—visiting a place is never the best way to see its true character—but if you can afford to move there, it's as nice a community of faggots as you'll find. And the visitors from San Francisco will keep you well supplied with fresh meat."

5. Coralville, Iowa

"Aside from being the location of one of the most perfect adult bookstore arcades (called Just Different Too) in the country, this town has no other claim to sexual fame. But it's proof of one of my longtime tenets: Sex is everywhere. Just because you live in Podunk doesn't mean your libido died at birth. And the owners of this store clearly know what they (or at least their customers) like."

6. **Hampstead Heath (London, England)**
"A beautiful park, well worth wandering across just for the relief from the insistent 'city-ness' of London; but also worth a trip for the rampant sexuality that has apparently been going on here since sometime in the last century. I've spent hours on my knees in the mud there, and finer kneeling-mud is not to be found anywhere on the planet, I assure you."

7. **Denver, Colorado**
"First, it has two first-rate bathhouses, each one far better than anything New York City can offer. (There's also a third, which I haven't visited.) The attitude at both places is friendly and sex-positive: a relief from the attitude often found in the coastal cities. Second, Denver is a city with a large Mexican population. Am I guilty of stereotyping Mexicans? Yes. I think they're one of the most gorgeous nationalities on the planet, and if it weren't for some of their machismo hang-ups, I would've moved to Mexico long ago."

8. **Hippie Hollow (Austin, Texas)**
"This is a traditionally nude beach on Lake Travis, twenty miles west of town, where the hillsides are crisscrossed with trails. With the mild climate in Texas, this is pretty much a year-round possibility, but it's Splash Day (in early May) that officially kicks off the season. I prefer to stay away from organized madhouses, so I've never been to Splash Day; but the rest of the year is quite festive enough for me. Oh, yes: The rest of Austin is worth investigating too. Universities, parks, bookstores—the only thing missing is a bathhouse."

9. **Sydney, Australia**
"I feel kind of silly recommending a city the size of Los Angeles. Of course, sex is available in a city with a couple of million men. So what else is new? But I like the Aussie character: the casual, laid-back attitude (enough to make Californians seem uptight!), the devotion to physical pleasures like sun and sand and sex—and, of

course, the foreskin. Lady Jane Beach and Obelisk Beach were my two favorite hangouts there, but the KKK Sauna is also heaven."

10. Madison, Wisconsin
"The University of Wisconsin (which anchors the west end of the State Street transit mall) has something like 50,000 students, and it's amazing how hardy they all seem to be. As soon as the temperature climbs to about forty degrees in the spring (and often, there'll be a forty-degree day in January), the boys break out their shorts and tank tops. State Street is one of the sexiest spots on the planet, largely, I think, because it's so unexpected. This is the sort of display you might expect to find on Castro Street or Key West. Not in Wisconsin."

5 Men It Would Have Been Better Not to Go Home With

1. Fritz Haarmann (1876-1924)
Otherwise known as the "Hanover Vampire," Haarmann spent much of his life in and out of trouble, for child molesting, public indecency, and lewd conduct. Then he met and fell under the spell of a young down-and-out male prostitute, Hans Grans. Grans had a violent temper and a passion for the macabre, and Haarmann was so in love with the boy that he could refuse him nothing. Working together between 1918 and 1924, the two of them murdered upward of fifty young men and boys in the city of Hanover, Germany. Grans chose the victims (in one case, he coveted a pair of pants a boy was wearing), and, as one newspaper later put it, all of the victims were literally "bitten to death." In most cases, the boys were lured to Haarmann's cookshop, where they were quickly overpowered and knocked to the floor. Haarmann and Grans then fell upon the victim's throat, eating the neck and part of the head while frantically stimulating each other to orgasm. The victim was usual-

ly still alive during much of the ordeal.

Because of his vocation as a butcher, Haarmann made hundreds of people in the city unwitting accessories to his cannibalism: After killing his victims, he butchered their bodies and sold the remains as meat pies, soup bones, steaks, sausages, and other cuts of meat. After World War I, the city was suffering from famine, and it was often noted with puzzlement that Haarmann's shop had a steady supply of fresh meat when other shops in the area had none. Haarmann and Grans were eventually apprehended and brought to trial; a third sometime accomplice was never caught. Grans received a sentence of life imprisonment, later commuted to twelve years. Haarmann was condemned to death by decapitation. After his execution, his brain was removed and sent to a university for a study into the criminally insane. Ulli Lommel's 1973 film *Tenderness of the Wolves,* produced by Rainer Werner Fassbinder, was inspired by Haarmann's case.

2. Dean Allen Corll (1940-1973)

To one of the people who knew him in Houston, Texas, Dean Allen Corll was "the nicest person you'll ever meet, with the most infectious smile you'll ever see." To another, he was a "nice, polite man who loved to be around kids." The 33-year-old Corll had served in the Army, once run a local candy store, and worked as an electrician for the Houston Lighting and Power Co. He was also the key figure behind one of the worst killing sprees, lasting from 1970 to 1973, in U.S. history. With the help of two teenage accomplices (who were paid from $5 to $10 for each victim they helped round up), Corll lured adolescent boys, most of them runaways, to glue- and paint-sniffing parties at his suburban home. Once there, the victims were drugged, gagged, stripped naked, and tied down to a specially constructed plywood "torture" plank. A plastic sheet was spread beneath the victims to catch their blood. Corll then raped and mutilated them. Some were tortured for days before Corll finally strangled them or shot them through the head with his .22 pistol or before they died of shock. Others were dispatched in as little as ten minutes. "It's probably safe to say," said one psychiatrist, "that after the first murder Corll saw it was easy to kill, and the rest of his victims were not people to him, they were like dolls." In all, police eventually uncovered the bodies of twenty-seven victims, though suspicions remain that there were more. (Corll once bragged that he had also done a fair amount of killing in California.) Corll's killing spree ended when one of his accomplices, a seventeen-year-old high school dropout, shot him to death in self-defense; Corll was apparently incensed when the boy brought home a fifteen-year-old female victim for a change.

3. John Wayne Gacy Jr. (1942-1994)
In 1968 Gacy was convicted of a sodomy charge involving a teenage boy; he was sentenced to ten years in prison but was paroled after eighteen months. In 1971 he was accused of raping a 27-year-old man, but charges were dropped when the defendant failed to show up in court. Then, in 1978, police traced a missing fifteen-year-old boy to Gacy's home in suburban Chicago. Shortly thereafter, the digging began. "The only thing they can get me for is running a funeral parlor without a license," Gacy quipped as police unearthed body after body from beneath his home.

Outwardly Gacy seemed an unlikely candidate for mass murderer. The owner of a small construction company, he earned over $200,000 a year and was a member of the Jaycees. In 1970 he became a Democratic precinct captain. He enjoyed dressing up as Pogo the Clown and entertaining children in charity shows at local hospitals, and he received awards for his many civic contributions. But slightly more than a year after the digging under his house began, Gacy was convicted of murdering more people than anyone else in U.S. history: thirty-three young men and boys, whom he had raped, tortured, and killed between January 1972 and December 1978. Police found most of the bodies, nine of them still unidentified, buried in a forty-foot crawlspace beneath the house. (Gacy's second wife, who divorced him in 1976, once complained about an unpleasant odor coming from underneath the house; he told her it was the smell of dead rats.) Some of the victims were slowly strangled with a tourniquet around their necks—Gacy liked to prolong his victim's agony. Others were savagely tortured, and Gacy leaned over them reading loudly from the Bible while they convulsed.

Gacy eventually confessed to the murders. But then, in 1982, while he was awaiting execution on Menard Prison's death row, he did a macabre about-face and told a newspaper interviewer that someone else must have put all of those bodies under his house. In the same interview Gacy desperately tried to portray himself as a gentle, kind, religious man. "I have never been a homosexual," he added. "My own doctors say just the opposite. They say I've got a strong hatred toward them." About his victims, he remarked: "When I read that nineteen of them were prostitutes, I ask: What happened to the family unit?"

For the fourteen years his conviction was under appeal, Gacy kept himself occupied in prison answering the hundreds of letters he received every month and taking up oil painting. His bizarre portraits—of himself, of clowns, of Jesus, Hitler, and other subjects—sometimes sold for thousands of dollars on the open market and often attracted celebrity collectors such as film director John Waters. One painting was planned for the cover of a rock album to be released by Columbia Records—until Columbia's parent company, Sony, got nervous and nixed the deal. In 1993, Gacy and his lawyers set up a special John Wayne Gacy 900-number, where, for $1.99 a minute, callers could hear the mass murderer muse about life and proclaim his innocence. Meanwhile, his lawyers continued their legal maneuvers to keep Gacy from being executed. Said the impatient father of the fifteen-year-old whose disappearance led police to Gacy's home to begin with, "I'll go down and pull the switch myself if they want me to."

The appeals finally ran out. On May 10, 1994, more than five hundred people gathered outside Gacy's prison to celebrate his execution. One magazine described the scene as a "boozy carnival." ("I think we should have got here at six o'clock, camped out, and got a decent buzz going," one spectator was overheard grumbling.) There were heated verbal skirmishes between the small, inevitable group that was there to protest the death penalty and the much larger crowd that had assembled to revel in the occasion.

Shortly after midnight Gacy was executed by lethal injection. It took him eighteen minutes to die.

His brain was removed and sent to the University of Chicago Medical Center for examination and research.

4. William G. Bonin (1947-1996)

Bonin, a husky, good-looking 34-year-old truck driver, was described by friends as having a hypnotic, dominating personality. He lived with his parents in a suburb of Los Angeles, was frequently unemployed, and attracted little attention to himself—until, in July 1980, he was arrested as the ringleader behind the so-called "Freeway Killings" in Los Angeles. Beginning in the mid 1970s, the bodies of numerous young men and boys, forty-four in all, were found alongside freeways in parts of Los Angeles County and neighboring Orange County. Bonin, a muscular drifter with a previous conviction for child molestation, was subsequently charged with twelve of the killings, though police clearly suspected his involvement in many more. (Bonin himself told a television newsman that he had killed at least twenty-one youths.) Three young accomplices, two of them teenagers, were charged with complicity in the murders. One later hanged himself in jail before the case went to trial.

According to testimony, Bonin, sometimes with friends, cruised the streets in his "death van" and picked up hitchhikers, hustlers, and other young men. Once inside the van, the victims were robbed, raped, brutally tortured, and, finally, put to death. Bonin then dumped their bodies beside various freeways in the Los Angeles area. His youngest victim was twelve. One thirteen-year-old boy was castrated before he died. Another victim was killed with an ice pick driven into his skull. Others were strangled with their T-shirts. And still another, a seventeen-year-old German tourist named Marcus Grabs, was stabbed seventy times. "I can only liken it to a rabid dog that has gone mad and does not know when to stop biting," one homicide investigator said of the Grabs killing. Bonin was convicted in ten of the murders; he later stood trial for four more. With mothers and other relatives of some of the victims sitting in the front row of the court, Judge William Keene sentenced him to death. In February 1996, Bonin was executed by lethal injection at San Quentin prison.

5. Jeffrey Dahmer (1960-1994)

On a suffocatingly hot night in July 1991, the people of Milwaukee watched in fascination as police removed murder evidence from a one-bedroom apartment in one of the more downscale sections of town. The evidence included a freezer full of human entrails, plastic bags full of bones, and a Crock-Pot with human penises in it. Also removed were a barrel full of human torsos, a refrigerated skull, and dozens of snapshots of mutilated and dismembered young men. By the next morning, everyone in America knew who Jeffrey Dahmer was and what he had done.

Dahmer—a soft-spoken and good-looking 31-year-old—had, as a teenager, tortured and dismembered animals. His first human victim was a hitchhiker in 1978 in Ohio. Dahmer was barely eighteen when he killed the boy, sodomized the corpse, and then cut the body into small pieces, which he scattered around the countryside. By the time he moved to Milwaukee, he had taken to picking up young men (most of them black) at gay bars, taking them back to his apartment, drugging them, killing them, and then having sex with their bodies. He also frequently cut up the bodies and preserved the parts to eat or masturbate with later. Some of the victims were skinned, filleted, and turned into bizarre tabletop sculptures that Dahmer kept throughout his apartment. Others were still alive, though unconscious, as Dahmer performed makeshift lobotomies on them (sometimes with a hand drill) in order to turn them into sex "zombies." One victim, a 14-year-old boy, managed to escape and fled down the street half naked and bleeding. He attracted the attention of the police, but Dahmer came running after him and explained that he and the boy were lovers and had just had a fight. The police drove off, and Dahmer dragged the boy back inside and butchered him that night.

Dahmer was eventually convicted of having murdered seventeen men and boys in all and was sentenced to 936 years in prison. At the sentencing some of the victims' relatives screamed obscenities at both Dahmer and the judge. Asked why he had committed such terrible acts, Dahmer replied, "I could completely control a person, a person that I found attractive, and keep them with me as long as possible, even if it meant just keeping a part of them." He also acknowledged that repressed homosexuality had had much to do with his problems. Homosexuality, he said, "was something that was to be kept hush-hush, not talked about, not even thought about. So I just kept it all within me and never talked about sexual issues at all, really, with anyone."

Three years into his prison sentence, Dahmer—who by then had become a born-again Christian—was beaten to death by a fellow inmate. "Now is everybody happy?" Dahmer's mother bitterly asked the press. "Now that he's bludgeoned to death, is that good enough for everyone?"

"I'm happy and very excited that the monster is finally dead," said the sister of one of Dahmer's victims.

23 Countries in Which Homosexual Acts Between Consenting Adults Have Been Decriminalized, and When

1. France 1810
2. Poland 1932
3. Denmark 1933
4. Switzerland 1942
5. Hungary 1961
6. Great Britain 1967
7. Germany 1969
8. Austria 1971
9. The Netherlands 1971
10. Norway 1972
11. Spain 1980
12. Scotland 1981
13. Northern Ireland 1982
14. New Zealand 1986
15. Belize 1988
16. Israel 1988
17. Hong Kong 1990
18. Ukraine 1991

19. Estonia 1992
20. Latvia 1992
21. Ireland 1993
22. Russia* 1993
23. Bermuda 1994

* Homosexual acts were first decriminalized in Russia in 1917 after the Revolution, then recriminalized under Stalin in 1934, then decriminalized again under Boris Yeltsin after the dissolution of the Soviet Union.

25 Countries in Which Homosexuality Is Still Specifically Proscribed by Law

1. Afghanistan
2. Cuba
3. Ecuador
4. Ethiopia
5. India
6. Iran
7. Jordan
8. Kenya
9. Kuwait
10. Lebanon
11. Libya
12. Morocco
13. Nepal
14. Nigeria
15. Pakistan
16. Romania
17. Western Samoa
18. Saudi Arabia
19. Singapore
20. South Africa
21. Sri Lanka
22. Syria
23. Uganda
24. Zaire
25. Zimbabwe

SOURCE: *The Third Pink Book: A Global View of Lesbian and Gay Oppression* by Hendriks, Tielman, and van der Veen (Prometheus Books, 1993)

26 Famous Men Who Were Arrested on Gay Sex or Morals Charges

1. Jacques de Molay (1243-1314), last grand master of the Knights Templars
2. Sandro Botticelli (1445-1510), Italian painter
3. Leonardo da Vinci (1452-1519), Italian painter and inventor
4. Nicholas Udall (1505-1556), English playwright
5. Marc Antoine Muret (1526-1586), French writer
6. Anthony Bacon (1558-1601), brother of Sir Francis Bacon
7. Jerome Duquesnoy (1602-1654), Flemish sculptor
8. Samuel Foote (1720-1777), English actor and playwright
9. Simeon Solomon (1840-1905), English painter
10. Oscar Wilde (1854-1900), Irish playwright and wit
11. Bill Tilden (1893-1953), U.S. tennis champion
12. Henry Cowell (1897-1965), U.S. composer
13. William Haines (1900-1973), U.S. film actor
14. Jean Genet (1910-1986), French writer
15. Sir John Gielgud (b. 1904), British actor
16. Alan Turing (1912-1954), English mathematician and computer science pioneer
17. Walter W. Jenkins (1918-1985), White House aide to President Johnson
18. Montgomery Clift (1920-1966), U.S. actor
19. G. Harrold Carswell (1920-1992), U.S. Supreme Court nominee
20. Pier Paolo Pasolini (1922-1975), Italian film director
21. Sergei Paradzhanov (1924-1993), Russian film director
22. George Maharis (b. 1928), U.S. actor
23. Jim Jones (1931-1978), U.S. cult leader
24. Robert Bauman (b. 1937), former U.S. congressman (R-Md.)
25. Daniel Curzon (b. 1939), U.S. writer
26. Jon Hinson (1942-1995), former U.S. congressman (R-Miss.)

The Stories Behind 14 of Those Arrests

1. Jacques de Molay (1243-1314), last grand master of the Knights Templars

The Knights Templars were a powerful religious-military order established at the time of the Crusades. Fear of their influence and a desire for their wealth prompted Philip IV of France to have them arrested en masse in 1308. They were charged with having committed sodomy and heresy. It was said that during initiation into the order new members were forced to kiss the anuses of their superiors and submit to homosexual intercourse. De Molay, grand master of the Templars, denied the charges of sodomy but eventually confessed, under torture, to having committed heresy. He was burned at the stake.

2. Leonardo da Vinci (1452-1519), Italian painter and inventor

Leonardo was twenty-four when he was arrested on charges of having had sex with a seventeen-year-old male prostitute. He was given a conditional discharge, but two months later the charges were renewed, and he was arrested again. He spent a short time in jail but was soon released, probably as a result of the intervention of highly placed friends.

3. Nicholas Udall (1505-1556), English playwright

Though best remembered today as the author of the first known English stage comedy, *Ralph Roister Doister,* Udall acquired a reputation of a different sort as a headmaster at Eton: He was overly fond of caning handsome young students. In 1541 he was imprisoned for having sex with two of his students and a servant. His incarceration lasted only a few months: His reputation as a playwright apparently helped him gain an early parole.

4. Simeon Solomon (1840-1905), English painter

Described by John Addington Symonds as "a distempered and radically vicious soul," Solomon was a prolific artist whose work was obsessively erotic and often explicitly homosexual in theme. Among his admirers were Algernon Swinburne and Oscar Wilde. In 1873, when he was only thirty-three, he was arrested for soliciting sex in a public lavatory in London. When he was found guilty, his friends and patrons deserted him. He ended his life, some thirty years later, as a destitute pavement artist, drawing sketches on the sidewalk and begging money from passersby.

5. Sir John Gielgud (b. 1904), British actor

In 1953 Gielgud was arrested on gay sex charges in London and was fined the equivalent of twenty dollars after pleading guilty to "importuning." (Apparently hoping to go unrecognized in court, he listed his occupation as "clerk.") Despite his standing as one of the greatest actors of the twentieth century, he was later, because of the arrest, denied an entrance visa to perform in the United States. At the time of the incident, entrapment of male homosexuals in public rest rooms was so widespread in London that the English physicist Derek Jackson wrote to a friend in France, "Never go to a public lavatory in London. I always pee in the street. You may be fined a few pounds for committing a nuisance, but in a public lavatory you risk two years in prison because a policeman in plain clothes says you smiled at him."

6. Alan Turing (1912-1954), English mathematician and computer science pioneer

A burglary at Turing's home led police to the discovery of his sexual involvement with a nineteen-year-old boy; Turing was arrested and charged with six counts of "gross indecency." Because of his international standing as a scientist, the court sentenced him to probation, but with the stipulation that he undergo medical treatment for his homosexuality. The treatment consisted of a series of female hormone injections to eliminate his libido—in other words, chemical castration. The injections left him impotent and caused him to grow feminine breasts; they also impaired his thinking. Barely two years after the arrest, and only a year after completing the court-ordered therapy, he committed suicide by eating an apple dipped in cyanide.

7. Walter W. Jenkins (1918-1985), White House aide to President Johnson

A longtime aide and close personal friend of Lyndon Johnson, Jenkins was forced to resign from his post as special assistant to the president after he was arrested in 1964 on charges of having committed homosexual acts in a YMCA two blocks from the White House. He had been arrested once before, in 1959, on the same charges at the same YMCA.

8. Montgomery Clift (1920-1966), U.S. actor

Shortly after Clift was nominated for an Academy Award for his performance in Fred Zinnemann's *The Search,* he was arrested for soliciting a young hustler on New York's 42nd Street. His lawyers kept the incident hushed up.

9. G. Harrold Carswell (1920-1992), U.S. Supreme Court nominee

Carswell was arrested in 1976 after allegedly soliciting a plainclothes police officer outside a shopping mall men's room in Tallahassee, Florida. In 1970 Carswell had been nominated to the Supreme Court by Richard Nixon; his nomination was rejected by the Senate because, among other things, he was regarded as an advocate of racial segregation. After his arrest in Florida, Carswell checked into a local psychiatric hospital. The rest room where he was arrested became a popular local tourist attraction and eventually had to be closed.

10. Sergei Paradzhanov (1924-1993), Russian film director

In 1974, Paradzhanov—best known to Western audiences for his critically acclaimed 1966 film *Shadows of Forgotten Ancestors*—was arrested by the KGB and charged with a wide variety of crimes, including "homosexuality," "speculation in foreign currency," "spreading venereal disease," and "speculation in art objects." Regarded as a dissenter by the Soviet government—which had condemned much of his work for its anti-Soviet tendencies—Paradzhanov was sentenced to five years' hard labor. Under pressure from international authorities, the Soviet government finally released him in 1978 but refused to allow him to make another film until 1985.

11. George Maharis (b. 1928), U.S. actor
The handsome star of the popular 1960s TV series *Route 66* was first arrested in 1967 in the rest room of a Hollywood restaurant and charged with "lewd conduct" after he allegedly solicited an undercover vice officer. Another arrest followed seven years later, in 1974, for "performing an act of oral copulation" with a 33-year-old male hairdresser in a gas station washroom in West Los Angeles. The charge was later reduced to "trespassing," and Maharis was fined $500 and given three years' probation.

12. Jim Jones (1931-1978), U.S. cult leader
Jones was arrested in 1973 for soliciting an undercover police officer at a gay porno theater in Los Angeles. The charges were later dropped. In 1978 he gained worldwide notoriety after engineering the mass murder-suicide of 913 of his followers at the so-called People's Temple in Guyana.

13. Robert Bauman (b. 1937), former U.S. congressman
Bauman was arrested in 1980 for soliciting sex with a sixteen-year-old boy. "I have been plagued by two afflictions," he told the press, "alcoholism and homosexual tendencies. But I do not consider myself a homosexual." As a conservative Republican from Maryland, Bauman had consistently voted against gay rights issues in the House of Representatives and was a vocal supporter of the Moral Majority. After his arrest he made repeated assertions that he was being cured of his "homosexual tendencies"; in August 1983, however, he finally came out and admitted he was gay. His wife of twenty-one years immediately had their marriage annulled. He has since gone into private practice as a lawyer, and in 1986 he wrote *The Gentleman from Maryland: The Conscience of a Gay Conservative,* a personal memoir in which he spoke of the need for legal changes to protect gay men and lesbians from discrimination and harassment.

14. **Jon Hinson (1942-1995), former U.S. congressman**
Hinson, a Republican representative from Mississippi, was arrested in 1976 for committing an obscene act at the Iwo Jima Memorial in Arlington, Virginia. In 1981 he was arrested again, this time in a House of Representatives men's room, and was charged with "oral sodomy" with a 28-year-old man. Hinson resigned from office shortly after his second arrest. He died of AIDS complications in 1995.

19 Prominent Individuals Who Supported the Idea of Homosexual Rights Before 1930

1. Jeremy Bentham (1748-1832), English philosopher and "father of Utilitarianism"
2. Martin Buber (1878-1965), Jewish religious philosopher
3. Sir Richard Burton (1821-1890), English explorer and author
4. Albert Einstein (1879-1955), German-U.S. physicist
5. Havelock Ellis (1859-1939), English sexologist
6. Sigmund Freud (1856-1939), Austrian founder of psychoanalysis
7. Emma Goldman (1869-1940), U.S. political activist
8. Hermann Hesse (1877-1962), German novelist
9. Karl Jaspers (1883-1969), German philosopher
10. Richard von Krafft-Ebing (1840-1902), German neuropsychiatrist
11. Thomas Mann (1875-1955), German author
12. Rainer Maria Rilke (1875-1926), German poet
13. Bertrand Russell (1872-1970), English philosopher
14. Margaret Sanger (1885-1960), founder of the U.S. birth control movement
15. George Bernard Shaw (1856-1950), British playwright

16. Leo Tolstoy (1828-1910), Russian author
17. Voltaire (1694-1778), French philosopher
18. H.G. Wells (1866-1946), English author
19. Emile Zola (1840-1902), French author

46 Celebrities Who Have Openly Supported Gay Rights

1. Maya Angelou
2. Edward Asner
3. Patty Duke Astin
4. Lauren Bacall
5. Joan Baez
6. Lucille Ball
7. Rona Barrett
8. Garth Brooks
9. Carol Burnett
10. Chip Carter
11. Kurt Cobain
12. Simone de Beauvoir
13. Phil Donahue
14. Jane Fonda
15. Gunter Grass
16. Hugh Hefner
17. Leona Helmsley
18. Coretta Scott King
19. Christopher Lee
20. Chris Evert Lloyd
21. Shirley MacLaine
22. Marsha Mason
23. Ethel Merman
24. Bette Midler
25. Elizabeth Montgomery
26. Paul Newman
27. Yoko Ono
28. Tom Petty
29. Martha Raye
30. Lynn Redgrave
31. Vanessa Redgrave
32. Maureen Reagan
33. Burt Reynolds
34. Joan Rivers
35. Jean-Paul Sartre
36. Cybill Shepherd
37. Neil Simon
38. Gloria Steinem
39. Elizabeth Taylor
40. Marlo Thomas
41. Abigail Van Buren
42. Nancy Walker
43. Dennis Weaver
44. James Woods
45. Joanne Woodward
46. Frank Zappa

18 Celebrity Homophobes

1. Rush Limbaugh (b. 1951) U.S. broadcast personality
Throughout his early career on radio, Limbaugh frequently insisted that gays used gerbils for sexual gratification ("I've checked it out with doctors at local hospitals, and it's absolutely true") and regularly made fun of people with AIDS, especially during a comedy segment of his radio show, the AIDS Update, which he introduced with the theme songs "I'll Never Love This Way Again" by Dionne Warwick and "Back in the Saddle Again" by Gene Autry. He vehemently opposed allowing gays in the U.S. military, and after a gay rights demonstration in New York City he lashed out at homosexuals in general: "I say to those of you of the leftist, militant, homosexual crowd—take it somewhere else. Get out of our schools. Get out of our churches. Take your deadly, sickly behavior and keep it to yourselves." Ironically, before Limbaugh achieved fame as a national conservative commentator, his closest adviser and mentor was a gay man, Norm Woodruff. "I keep waiting," one of Limbaugh's former associates told an interviewer, "for Rush to say, 'You can't call me a homophobe because my career, in essence, was made by a homosexual.' Either I have a misunderstanding of how important Woodruff was to Rush, or there's something Rush doesn't want to talk about. It's kind of a mystery to me."

2. Buju Banton (b. 1973), Jamaican reggae-rap singer
The title track from his 1992 album, *Boom Bye Bye,* contained the lyrics "Faggots have to run/Or get a bullet in the head/Bang-bang in a faggot's head/Homeboys don't condone nasty men/They must die." The song, which included a background of firing guns, urged listeners to "get an automatic or an Uzi" and start murdering homosexuals. A spokeswoman for the singer insisted that the lyrics were "a product of his environment, not a reflection of his personal convictions." However, Banton himself defended the song, explaining that homosexuality "runs contrary to my religious beliefs."

3. Nancy Reagan (b. 1923), former first lady
Despite her close relationship with gay astrologer Carroll Righter as well as friendships with Roy Cohn and Truman Capote, Reagan denounced homosexuality as an "abnormality" and a "sickness" and claimed she could never vote for a political candidate who was gay. ("In order to hold office, you have to be a terribly strong man emotionally," she explained.) "Women's liberation and gay liberation [are] part of the same thing," she told an interviewer in 1981, "a weakening of the moral standards of this nation. It is appalling to see parades in San Francisco and elsewhere proclaiming 'gay pride' and all that. What in the world do they have to be proud of?" Her 1989 memoir, *My Turn*—a 384-page chronicle of her eight years as first lady—contained numerous, lengthy descriptions of her luncheons with Raisa Gorbachev ("blinis with caviar, cabbage rolls, blueberry pie, cookies, chocolates") but mentioned AIDS only once, and that in connection with Rock Hudson's attendance at a White House dinner ("I remember sitting across from him and thinking, *Gee, he's thin.* I asked him if he had been dieting").

4. Pope John Paul II (b. 1920)
In 1986 he proclaimed that "those who behave in a homosexual fashion...shall not enter the kingdom of God." A year later he publicly suggested that AIDS might indeed be God's punishment of homosexuals. In 1994 he told Italian pharmacists to stop selling condoms, which he said only encouraged immorality. A short time later he reiterated his belief that "a relationship between two men or two women cannot make up a real family."

5. L. Ron Hubbard (1911-1986), founder of Scientology
In his book *Dianetics,* Hubbard denounced homosexuality as an "illness" and a "perversion" and concluded that homosexuals were "extremely dangerous to society." He wrote: "A society which would continue to endure perversion and all its sad and sordid effects doesn't deserve to survive."

6. Ernest Hemingway (1899-1961), U.S. writer
He admitted he had "certain prejudices against homosexuality." He

also admitted that the whole subject bitterly depressed him. According to his longtime friend matador Sidney Franklin, Hemingway once spotted a man he thought was gay walking on the other side of the street in a town in Spain. "Watch this," Hemingway told Franklin. He walked across the street, wordlessly punched the man in the face, and then, with a satisfied grin on his face, just as wordlessly rejoined Franklin. "I know they are supposed to be amusing," he wrote of homosexuals in his second novel, *The Sun Also Rises,* "and you should be tolerant, but I wanted to swing on one, any one, anything to shatter that superior, simpering composure." Hemingway rejected Gertrude Stein's advice that he should pity, not hate, homosexuals and angrily told her she was "queer and liked only queers." After their friendship ended bitterly, Hemingway began publicly disparaging Stein as "a woman who isn't a woman."

7. Barbara Cartland (b. 1901), British romance novelist
In the late 1980s Cartland joined with a number of other prominent British authors—notably, Frederick Forsyth and Jeffrey Archer—in a campaign to keep mainstream British bookstores from stocking gay- and lesbian-themed titles. She denounced gay literature in general as "foul" and told the press, "These titles could easily pollute children's minds." She called for a boycott of all stores in Britain that sold gay books.

8. Ayn Rand (1905-1982), U.S. writer
She supported the repeal of laws prohibiting homosexual acts among consenting adults but qualified that support with the conviction that homosexuality was "utterly disgusting." Her own brother-in-law, to whom she was very close, was gay.

9. Andy Rooney (b. 1919), U.S. television personality
In 1990 Rooney said he "felt sorry" for gays. "I still don't think it's normal," he explained. "I think that homosexuality is inherently dangerous." He also stated that sodomy was "repugnant" and "in bad taste." A year earlier, on a CBS television special, he asserted that homosexual unions "lead quite often to premature death." "I feel the same way about homosexuals as I do about cigarette smok-

ers," he once remarked. "I wouldn't want to spend much time in a small room with one..." His comments, along with some questionable remarks about African-Americans, led to his being suspended from *60 Minutes* for three months. However, he returned to the air after barely a month: The show's ratings had dropped precipitously during his absence.

10. John Wayne (1907-1979), U.S. actor
In a 1976 *Advocate* interview, Wayne told interviewer Steve Warren, "So I see no reason to jump with joy because somebody is a gay, and I don't see any reason for waving a flag for all the wonderful things gays have done for the world...any more than you'd say, 'Oh, boy, hooray for the tuberculosis victim!' It's abnormal to me."

11. Edith Wharton (1862-1937), U.S. writer
She despised lesbians, whom she described as "appalling," and once warned a female friend visiting Paris that, whatever else happened, "you must never go near [Natalie Barney]." Although she maintained an amiable relationship with André Gide and had deep regard for the work of Marcel Proust (while being fully aware of his proclivities), she felt that homosexuals were "degenerates." In later years, as she became increasingly conservative in her religious beliefs, she often decried what she saw as the growing immorality of America, especially any blurring of the distinctions between the sexes.

12. Elvis Presley (1935-1977), U.S. entertainer
Even though he often paid lesbians to perform sexually for him, the self-described "king of the badasses" feared and detested gay men. Whenever he used public rest rooms, he had bodyguards stand watch outside the doors, in part because of a lifelong horror of homosexuals cruising him.

13. Hedda Hopper (1890-1966), U.S. gossip columnist
Although she befriended numerous gay men in her private life, Hopper publicly railed against homosexuality and "faggots," as she called them, and often equated society's growing sexual permissiveness with the rise of Communism. A staunch Republican, she once

hinted that Noël Coward and Democratic presidential candidate Adlai Stevenson were having an affair, and in 1963 she was sued by Elizabeth Taylor's second husband, Michael Wilding, for suggesting that he and Stewart Granger were lovers. (Hopper and her publisher settled out of court.) She felt it was her duty to expose homosexual activities within the film industry, even though her own manager was a well-known lesbian.

14. Rupert Murdoch (b. 1931), Australian-born media mogul
Murdoch told an interviewer in 1980, "I don't believe in the gay movement.... I think they should stay to themselves, just climb back into the cupboards.... I don't believe they are gay at all, they are very unhappy."

15. Dylan Thomas (1914-1953), Welsh poet
Thomas loathed homosexuals and denounced them as "willing-buttocked, celluloid-trousered degenerates." "It is the only vice, I think, that revolts me and makes me misanthropic," he once wrote a friend.

16. Field Marshal Bernard Montgomery (1887-1976), British war hero
He regularly ranted against homosexuality, which he despised as "unnatural," "evil," and "utterly wrong." He actively opposed the campaign to decriminalize homosexual acts in Britain in the 1960s after the release of the Wolfenden Report. "I have heard some say...that such practices are allowed in France and other NATO countries," he proclaimed in a speech before Parliament. "We are not French, and we are not other nationals. We are British, thank God!" He warned that repealing the sodomy laws would corrupt "the moral fiber of the youth of this nation."

17. Ken Kesey (b. 1935), U.S. writer
In a 1986 interview in *Esquire* magazine, the author of *One Flew Over the Cuckoo's Nest* said that the homosexuals he knew were neither happy nor proud and speculated that AIDS might be caused not by a virus but simply by homosexual acts themselves. "It seems

to me," he remarked, "it's one's job to put sperm in a place that's designed for it." Referring to homosexuals in general, he said, "I'll bet you water in hell that when we tally up our beans at the end of the game, our good beans and our bad beans, that I've got more good beans than they do. I mean, why not go down the road that gives the most good beans?"

18. The U.S. Olympic Committee

In 1982 the United States Olympic Committee sued organizers of San Francisco's Gay Olympics claiming that the USOC had exclusive use of the word *olympics* and that the name Gay Olympics infringed on their copyright. They sought and received an injunction barring use of the name Gay Olympics. Gay organizers argued, unsuccessfully, that more than a dozen other "olympics"—including the Special Olympics, the International Police Olympics, the Armenian Olympics, the Crab-Cooking Olympics, the Eskimo Olympics, and the Rat Olympics—had gone on for years unchallenged by the USOC. Not only was the USOC's position upheld in court, but also organizers of the Gay Olympics were eventually ordered to pay the USOC $96,000 in legal fees. The decision was appealed to the Supreme Court, which in June 1987 ruled against the Gay Olympics, which are now known as the Gay Games.

Ordinary People: 8 Gay Men Who Were Brutally Murdered

1. Martin Coetzee

Coetzee was a well-known hairdresser in his hometown of Bloemfontein, South Africa. He was found dead in his apartment on Christmas Eve, 1973; he had been strangled to death with a necktie. Police arrested nineteen-year-old Coenraad Kroukamp, who claimed that Coetzee had plied him with liquor and then made sexual advances toward him. The boy's attorney argued in court, "Although the deceased has been described as a soft-natured person of slight build, he was nevertheless an experienced adult man who had forced himself on a young, healthy man half his age. Who can say what the psychological effect would have been on this young man had the deceased succeeded in his intentions?" Though there were many irregularities in the boy's story—for example, by his own admission he did not at first resist Coetzee's advances—he was acquitted of murder on the grounds that he had acted in self-defense. "It must be accepted," ruled the judge, "that a normal man in his position…was entitled to defend himself."

2. Richard Heakin

Heakin, a 21-year-old microfilm technician from Lincoln, Nebraska, was killed by four teenage boys outside a gay bar in Tucson, Arizona, on June 6, 1976. The boys were part of a larger group of teenagers harassing gay men leaving the disco at closing time. Heakin was standing by a car talking to friends when he was attacked and knocked down. Police said his death was caused by a severe blow, perhaps a hard kick, to the back of the head. After the four boys who attacked him were caught and arrested (based on information supplied by witnesses), they confessed to the crime and admitted they had been out drinking beer and looking "to beat up queers." However, despite their confessions, superior court judge Ben C. Birdsall refused to hand down jail sentences of any kind in the case. Characterizing the youths as "worthwhile members of the community," he stressed that they were all high school athletes and that "none of them use drugs or even marijuana." He gave them probation and dismissed suggestions that they at least undergo psychiatric counseling. "The four youths and their parents have been punished enough," he explained.

3. Robert Hillsborough

On the night of June 21, 1977, Hillsborough, a 33-year-old city gardener, was stabbed to death on a San Francisco street by a group of men who screamed, "Faggot! Faggot!" as they knocked him down and repeatedly drove a knife into him. His killers had followed him from a nearby hamburger stand, where they spotted him coming home from a date with a boyfriend. Hillsborough was stabbed a total of fifteen times in the chest and face. Of the four men who were eventually arrested in connection with the killing, one was convicted of second-degree murder; another, a juvenile, was convicted of assault; a third received immunity for testifying against the first; and the fourth was convicted of felonious assault. Hillsborough's mother consequently filed a $5-million civil rights lawsuit against the killers. Also named in the lawsuit was Anita Bryant who, Mrs. Hillsborough asserted, had conspired to deprive her son of his civil rights. Mrs. Hillsborough contended that Bryant and other antigay zealots, through their inflammatory rhetoric, had created an atmosphere of homophobic hysteria that contributed to her son's murder. (Only weeks before the killing, for example, Bryant had told a large audience of her followers that homosexuals were "human garbage.") Informed of the lawsuit, Bryant commented, "I had nothing to do with any murders. There is a homosexual murder every day in San Francisco…my conscience is clear." Mrs. Hillsborough's lawsuit was eventually dismissed by the courts.

4. Wayne Lee

On the night of March 25, 1979, Wayne Lee, a 33-year-old beauty pageant judge, was savagely beaten in a vacant garage in downtown Savannah, Georgia. The men who attacked him were three U.S. Army Rangers. According to one witness, Lee pleaded for his life and begged the men, "Don't hurt me," while they repeatedly kicked, struck, and stomped on him. Lee later died in a hospital without regaining consciousness. The attending physician testified in court, "This was probably the most mutilated person I have ever seen still alive." Lee, he said, was "almost unrecognizable as a human being" when he was brought into the emergency room that night. An attorney for the Army Rangers argued that Lee had provoked the attack by making homosexual advances toward the three men at a nearby adult bookstore. He urged the jury to "place the responsibility where it lies" and characterized the defendants as "young, foolish, clean-cut, and honest." Although the defendants could have been convicted of murder or manslaughter, the jury instead convicted them of a misdemeanor offense: simple battery, the least possible charge for which a conviction could have been returned. Superior court judge Perry Brannen Jr. sentenced the men to a maximum of twelve months in jail but left open the possibility that the sentences could be modified to include some kind of community service instead.

5. Fred Paez

In the early morning hours of June 28, 1980, Paez was shot to death in the back of the head. His killer was an off-duty Houston police officer, Kevin McCoy. At the time, Officer McCoy and a friend were working as security guards in the city's warehouse district; they later admitted that between the two of them they had consumed three six-packs of beer the night of the shooting. McCoy testified that Paez, a 27-year-old gay activist, had made sexual advances toward them, including offers of oral sex, and then had tried to fondle him. He claimed that a scuffle ensued and that his .45 automatic pistol went off accidentally, shooting Paez through the back of the skull. Despite McCoy's assertion that the shooting had been accidental, a ballistics expert later testified, "This weapon does not go off automatically." McCoy was indicted by a grand jury on charges of negligent homicide but was subsequently acquitted. Officially, Paez's killing was ruled an "accidental" death.

6. Charles Howard

Twenty-three-year-old Charles Howard was known as "Gentle Charlie" to his friends in Bangor, Maine. A slightly built, rather effeminate young man, he was killed on the night of July 7, 1984. He and a friend were walking home from a church meeting when they were attacked by three teenage boys, one of whom had suggested to the other two, "Hey, let's kick the shit out of this fag!" Howard tried to run away but tripped over a curb. The three teenagers fell upon him and started kicking and beating him. Then they picked him up and, despite his terrified pleas of "No, no! I can't swim!" tossed him over a bridge into a stream, where he drowned. The teenage killers were arrested after they bragged to a friend about what they had done. Originally charged with first-degree murder, they were eventually convicted on charges of manslaughter—a charge of manslaughter legally implies that they did not act out of malice—and were sentenced by the court to incarceration at a youth center in Portland. All three boys were released by their twenty-first birthdays.

7. Harry Wayne Watson

Watson, a 35-year-old Kalamazoo, Michigan, man, was sitting by a stream under a train trestle when he was attacked by two drunken teenagers, aged seventeen and nineteen, who kicked and beat him unconscious on the night of May 25, 1985. The boys claimed that Watson had offered them blow jobs and had groped one of them. (Watson's friends later said that such behavior would have been "completely out of character" for him.) After the initial attack, the two boys, who were reportedly covered with blood, went off to a party and left Watson, unconscious but alive, under the trestle. They returned an hour later with a third boy and a sledgehammer. Their intention was to "finish off" Watson. The gay man was lying senseless where they had left him.

According to testimony, the seventeen-year-old raised the sledgehammer over Watson's head and drove it down as hard as he could three times into Watson's skull. He later bragged to friends that he had killed a "fag" and was consequently arrested. At the trial an attorney tried to portray Watson as "an aggressive, perverted homosexual who was down there to attack young boys." The jury, which held a prayer meeting before beginning deliberations, took less than two hours to return a verdict exonerating the seventeen-year-old of all charges. In a rare move, the presiding judge publicly disagreed with their verdict. "This is the first time in almost twelve years on the bench," he stated, "that I felt I would strongly have differed with the jury. I would have found first-degree murder." Ironically, the two other boys had already pleaded guilty to charges related to the killing.

8. Julio Rivera

Rivera was a 29-year-old gay bartender from the South Bronx. On the night of July 2, 1990, he was bludgeoned to death by youths wielding a hammer and a plumber's wrench at a well-known gay cruising area in Queens. His killers—21-year-old Erik Brown and 19-year-old Esat Bici—were arrested shortly afterward when they boasted to friends that they had killed a gay man. The two later acknowledged that they had gone out that night to beat up a "homo."

At the trial, defense attorneys attempted to portray Rivera as a promiscuous gay man who was out cruising and putting the community at risk for AIDS. However, in contrast to similar other trials, the jury didn't yield to that kind of reasoning: They found Brown and Bici guilty, and the two youths were sentenced to twenty-five years to life in prison for murder.

After the sentence was read, Bici's aunt, incensed by the decision against her nephew, stood outside the courtroom screaming antigay slurs and threats. "It's about time we started picking on them!" she complained of homosexuals. "They have special privileges, but we're real people, people that didn't lose any chromosomes!" As the murder victim's former gay lover exited the courtroom, Bici and Brown's friends taunted him with cries of, "Put on your lipstick, honey!" (Earlier, during the trial, they had baited gay spectators by calling them "faggots.") One defense attorney bitterly denounced the verdict and the sentence. The jury, he angrily complained, had caved in to "the desires of the gay rights activists" and had promoted "the furtherance of the 'No gay bashing' doctrine they espoused."

2 Famous Men Who Were Victims of Gay Bashings

1. Tennessee Williams (1911-1983), **U.S. playwright**

Williams and a friend were walking home late at night from a popular gay bar in Key West in January 1979 when they were jumped by five teenage boys who began to beat them. Williams's friend tried to run, but the playwright—knocked to the ground and searching for his glasses in the melee—declared, "I am not in the habit of retreat!" Neither man was seriously injured, but less than a week later a gang of teenage boys stood outside Williams's house chanting, "Come on out, faggot!" while tossing firecrackers and beer cans at his windows. Both episodes were part of an ongoing epidemic of antigay violence that had occurred on the island after a local Baptist minister ran an ad in the Key West newspaper suggesting, "If I were the chief of police, I would get me a hundred good men, give them each a baseball bat, and have them walk down Duval Street and dare one of these freaks to stick his head over the sidewalk. That is the way it was done in Key West in the days I remember and love." Said one Key West resident: "In most small towns they realize that if a famous person is hurt there, there are worldwide repercussions: Your town gets known as the place where so and so was hurt.... Tennessee Williams is one of the great tourist attractions in Key West. You would think the...city would see that he is comfortable here, safe here, can work here." Williams himself remained philosophical about the attacks. "There is violence everywhere," he told a reporter.

2. Dick Button (b. 1929), **U.S. figure skater**

Button, a two-time Olympic gold medalist in figure skating, was bludgeoned by a gang of teenagers wielding baseball bats in Central Park on the night of July 5, 1978. According to one of the teenagers, all of whom were later arrested and charged with assault and robbery, "We went out to get faggots because we hate them." Button and the five other victims were in the park shortly after nine o'clock, when the attackers came through swinging baseball bats, large tree branches, and a furniture leg. All six of the victims sustained skull fractures from the assault. Button also suffered serious nerve damage and permanent hearing loss in one ear. According to police, the attackers, once in custody, bragged openly about what they'd done and boasted they would do it again if given the opportunity.

7 Movies That in Some Way Deal With Homosexuality, and What the Mainstream Critics Said About Each

1. ***The Boys in the Band*** **(1970)**
The film: Mart Crowley's play—the most famous of all plays about homosexuality—was first performed on the New York stage in April 1968. Crowley himself produced and wrote the screenplay for the 1970 film version. The film starred the original off-Broadway cast and was directed by William Friedkin, who later directed *The French Connection* and *The Exorcist.* The story is about a gathering of nine men—eight gay and one who insists he's not—at a birthday party, where, to varying degrees, they bare their souls.

What the critics said: The Boys in the Band broke new ground in tackling a formerly taboo subject on the screen—the private lives of homosexuals. But while theater critics had almost unanimously praised the stage play, the film received decidedly mixed reviews. Hollis Alpert, in *Saturday Review,* called it "an indulgence of truly extraordinary masochism, and one which all too neatly reveals the various hang-ups and self-hatreds of the participants in the party. Guilt eventually undoes [almost] everyone...."

Joseph Morgenstern, in *Newsweek,* labeled it "gross" and "irrevocably ungay." He wrote: "To convince us that homosexuals hate themselves, it generates so much self-hate that the movie itself turns hateful."

Critic George N. Boyd, writing in *The Christian Century,* praised the film for its tight construction, humor, and pathos but noted, "The story might have been better balanced if at least one of the eight had advanced a cogent argument for the normalcy of homosexuality."

Pauline Kael wrote in *The New Yorker:* "William Friedkin brings out the worst of the play with guilt-ridden pauses and long see-the-suffering-in-the-face closeups. Every blink and lick of the lips has its rigidly scheduled meaning, and it's all so solemn—like Joan Crawford when she's thinking."

John Gruen in *Vogue* was one of the few critics to praise the film. He thought it was "explosive," "even better than the play," and called it "the best, most searing, and funniest look into the 'gay' life."

And critic Frank Rich, in *Time,* concluded: "If the situation of the homosexual is ever to be understood by the public, it will be because of the breakthrough made by this humane, moving picture."

Epilogue: Reacting to criticism from gays that the movie presented a distorted view of gay men as hostile and self-destructive and that it only reinforced conventional, negative stereotypes, Friedkin told one interviewer, "The film is not about homosexuality. It's about human problems. I hope there are happy homosexuals. There just don't happen to be any in my film."

2. ***Death in Venice*** **(1971)**

The film: Among the directors who had tried and failed over the years to bring Thomas Mann's novella *Death in Venice* to the screen were John Huston, Joseph Losey, and Jose Ferrer. It was Italian film director Luchino Visconti who finally succeeded, though not without difficulties. Mann's story—about a disillusioned middle-aged artist who becomes obsessed with a beautiful fourteen-year-old boy during a vacation to Venice—scared off numerous producers, who refused to finance the project. One Italian producer was willing to back the movie, but only if Visconti turned the fourteen-year-old boy into a Lolita-style adolescent nymphet. Finally Warner Bros., which had released Visconti's *The Damned* in 1969 (and had made money doing it), agreed to finance the film and gave Visconti a free hand in directing it.

What the critics said: After *Death in Venice* had its world premiere in London in 1971, the critics pounced, with vehemence and indignation. Visconti had made several changes from the novella. First and foremost, he had changed the book's central character, Aschenbach, from a writer to a composer. He also added several flashback scenes, which awkwardly attempted to clarify Aschenbach's character. But perhaps most galling to some critics was that the homosexual implications of the story seemed more pointed in the film than they did in the book. The critics went on the defensive, often suggesting that the movie was some kind of sordid homosexual fantasy concocted by the "flamboyantly" homosexual Visconti.

Stefan Kanfer wrote in *Time:* "Mann's *Death in Venice* is, in fact, no more about homosexuality than Kafka's *The Metamorphosis* is about entomology.... This film is worse than mediocre; it is corrupt and distorted...it is irredeemably, unforgivably gay."

Saturday Review's Hollis Alpert wrote: "To simply have Aschenbach turn queer, to have him pursue Tadzio as though in search of forbidden erotic pleasure, amounts to a gross distortion of Mann's meaning. Even more vulgar is the camera's fixation on the boy's buttocks, an implication that Aschenbach is a budding sodomite."

Paul D. Zimmerman disdainfully dismissed the film in *Newsweek* as "a requiem for an aging homosexual."

National Review's David Brudnoy called it "a high-fashion exploitation drag."

There were exceptions to the general indignation.

Penelope Gilliatt in *The New Yorker* described *Death in Venice* as a film "of unearthly beauty.... It is plainly the work of a great man."

Rex Reed in *Holiday* concluded that it "is not a masterpiece without reservations, but it is a very compelling and distinguished piece of art."

And in the *London Sunday Times,* critic Dilys Powell wrote: "In the past quarter of a century there have been films potentially more influential.... I can think of none which has been more truly a work of art."

Epilogue: Critical appreciation of Visconti's film has steadily increased since its premiere in 1971. It is now justifiably regarded by many as Visconti's masterpiece.

3. *La Cage aux Folles* (1978)

The film: Directed by Edouard Molinaro and written by Francis Veber, who later wrote the screenplay for the American comedy *Partners, La Cage aux Folles* was based on a long-running French stage play. For the movie, Ugo Tognazzi and Michel Serrault took the roles of two gay lovers, Renato and Albin, who own a fashionable Saint-Tropez nightclub featuring female impersonators. Albin is the club's star performer. When Laurent, Renato's son from a long-ago heterosexual encounter, announces he is going to be married, the two lovers try to act straight for their meeting with the bride's austere, moralistic family. Albin, in drag, pretends to be Laurent's mother—with disastrous results. But there is a happy ending.

What the critics said: La Cage aux Folles caught most critics off-guard; it was a sleeper hit. Though the film opened in New York in the spring of 1979, most critics paid little or no attention to it, and some of those who did didn't write reviews until as late as August.

Brendan Gill wrote in *The New Yorker:* "We laugh almost without stop at the increasingly frantic means by which Renato and Albin seek to transform themselves for Laurent's sake, but little by little something much more interesting than mere farce emerges from the slapstick somersaultings of the plot; we begin to find Albin and Renato affecting as well as amusing. For they have put their lives in jeopardy to please a boy and girl unworthy of them; the more chances they take, the more our hearts go out to them."

Newsweek's David Ansen wrote: "The clockwork formulas—and the image of homosexuals as swishy queens—are old-fashioned, but Tognazzi and Serrault manage to invest their parts with great comic zest and delicate pathos." The film, he said, was "laugh-out-loud funny."

Richard Schickel wrote in *Time:* "Though the gays must make eccentric adjustments to the exigencies of living, their behavior is viewed as no more unusual than the quirks everyone develops to get through the day as pleasantly as possible." He called the film "the warmest comedy of the year...giddy, unpretentious, and entirely lovable."

Critic Robert Hatch of *The Nation* liked the film but had reservations about it: "*La Cage aux Folles* capitalizes on the kind of hysterical exhibitionism that serious-minded homosexuals repudiate. The film is funny enough, if you're not in the line of fire, but I'm not prepared to say that the fun is entirely harmless."

One of the only critics to pan it outright was Vincent Canby in *The New York Times*. "*La Cage aux Folles,*" he wrote, "is naughty in the way of comedies that pretend to be sophisticated but actually serve to reinforce the most popular conventions and most witless stereotypes." He condemned it as foolish and mechanical. "Even worse, though," he wrote, "is the awful sentimentality."

Epilogue: With grosses in excess of $40 million, *La Cage aux Folles* became the highest-grossing foreign film of all time, a distinction it held until 1986. It was nominated for several Academy Awards, including for best director and best screenplay adapted from another medium, and spawned two sequels and a hit Broadway musical.

4. *Cruising* (1980)

The film: Directed by William Friedkin, who had directed *The Boys in the Band* a decade earlier, *Cruising* was based on a 1970 Gerald Walker novel about a series of gruesome murders within New York's gay S/M community. Al Pacino played a heterosexual cop who immerses himself in gay life in order to bait and trap the killer. In the process of tracking the murderer, he becomes troubled about his own sexual identity. The movie had barely started location shooting on the streets of New York when it became the object of daily protests by gay activists, who insisted that, by focusing on the S/M scene, the film would foster distorted attitudes among straight people about gay life and would trigger antigay violence. To ease some of their concerns, Friedkin put a brief disclaimer at the beginning of the film suggesting that his depiction of New York's gay S/M community was not meant to be representative of the gay community as a whole. It was not enough. A single unsolved murder at the end of the film still left many viewers with the impression that Pacino himself had become a brutal killer simply after being exposed to gay life.

What the critics said: Critics were almost unanimous in their condemnation of the film.

Vincent Canby wrote in *The New York Times:* "Homosexual activist groups, which have been protesting the production of *Cruising* on the grounds that it would present a distorted view of homosexual life, were right. *Cruising* is a homosexual horror film."

Time magazine critic Frank Rich noted that "*Cruising* is not antigay any more than a film like *American Gigolo* is antiheterosexual." He nonetheless described the film as "hopelessly fouled up…defeated by narrative loopholes, unconvincing plot twists…. This detective drama has something to offend almost everyone."

David Ansen wrote in *Newsweek:* "What Friedkin's film is about is anybody's guess. If he just wanted to make a thriller, he has made a clumsy and unconvincing one. If he wanted to explore the psychology of his characters, he has left out most of the relevant information. If he intended to illuminate the tricky subject of S/M, he hasn't even scratched the surface." He dismissed much of the film as "a superficially shocking tableau for the titillation and horror of his audience."

Roger Angell, in *The New Yorker,* wrote: "The picture goes on to suggest that homosexuality is catching and inescapably brutal: If you hang around with gays and the leather set, you will end up dead or killing someone. No one is immune—not an upright heterosexual cop, not a quiet, unaggressive homosexual bystander. Being gay is a dangerous business. This is a shocking conclusion for any movie to come to…."

Epilogue: Despite the protests and various calls for a boycott, *Cruising* grossed an impressive $5 million in its first five days of release. However, the grosses soon plummeted, and the movie eventually bombed. One major hitch in its distribution occurred when the largest theater chain in the country, the General Cinema Corporation, refused to honor its advance bookings of the film; the GMC claimed that because of the film's explicit scenes of sadomasochistic sex, *Cruising* should have been rated "X" instead of "R" and was therefore unsuitable for distribution to its theaters.

5. *Making Love* (1982)
The film: Making Love—the story of a young married doctor who comes to realize he is gay and who leaves his devoted wife—was one of the first major Hollywood releases to try presenting a non-hysterical, reasonably positive view of gay life. It was directed by Arthur Hiller (who had directed *Love Story*) and was released on Valentine's Day 1982. The screenplay was by Barry Sandler, based on a story from A. Scott Berg. The film starred Michael Ontkean as the doctor, Kate Jackson as his wife, and Harry Hamlin as the gay novelist with whom the doctor has his first homosexual affair.

What the critics said: Most critics praised the film's good intentions while often deploring what they saw as its naive and simplistic characterizations and conclusions.

Time's Richard Schickel wrote: "The people who made this picture are not interested in tragedy or even human messiness. They are determined to prove not only that 'nice boys do' but that homosexuals can be as well-adjusted and as middle-class as anyone else."

Stanley Kauffmann wrote in *The New Republic:* "Care has been taken to sanitize the script. The troubled husband and wife are childless. The male lovers are a doctor and a novelist, and the job the doctor gets in New York is at the Sloan-Kettering Institute. (No one who's working to cure cancer can be all bad, can he, even if he's homosexual?)"

David Ansen wrote in *Newsweek:* "Like other 'pioneering' Hollywood movies about minorities (*Gentleman's Agreement, Guess Who's Coming to Dinner*), the minority in question is presented in terms wholesome enough to win a Good Housekeeping Seal of Approval.… Still, one must applaud the attempt to reverse sexual stereotypes, however banal the results."

Lindsy Van Gelder wrote in *Ms.:* "*Making Love* unquestionably represents a long-overdue Hollywood breakthrough—if only because it validates up to now invisible gay lives." However, she noted, "most of the movie isn't a whole lot deeper than *General Hospital*."

Critic Judith Crist called it "simple-minded, soapy, and sappy," and Leonard Maltin dismissed it as "bland."

Janet Maslin, in *The New York Times,* described it as "a thoroughly old-fashioned, wonderfully sudsy romance" and wrote that much of it was "rip-roaring awful in an entirely enjoyable way."

Epilogue: Making Love grossed only $12 million at the box office.

6. *Maurice* (1987)

The film: After making the Oscar-winning box-office hit *A Room With a View* just two years before, director James Ivory and producer Ismail Merchant decided to take a chance on filming the most controversial and commercially venturesome of E.M. Forster's novels, *Maurice,* a story of homosexual love at the turn of the century. There were problems from the start. Investors who had been eager to finance *A Room With a View* suddenly shied away from a gay-themed film. Ruth Prawer Jhabvala, who had done the screenplays for most of Merchant and Ivory's previous films, refused to write the screenplay for *Maurice,* ostensibly because she thought the book was "flawed." Julian Sands, the male lead in *A Room With a View,* originally agreed to play the title role but then suddenly bowed out for "personal reasons." (He was replaced by a relative unknown, James Wilby.) There were even admonitions from various quarters that it was inappropriate to make "a salute to homosexual passion" in the midst of the AIDS epidemic. Nonetheless, Merchant and Ivory—whose own relationship has lasted over thirty years—persevered. The finished film costarred Hugh Grant and Rupert Graves, with several smaller character roles filled by such distinguished actors as Ben Kingsley, Denholm Elliott, and Simon Callow

What the critics said: When *Maurice* opened in 1987, the critics were almost unanimous in their praise.

Peter Travers, writing in *People,* called it "literate, passionate, impeccably acted and directed…a marvel of a movie." "Only the best films," he noted, "create a world so richly textured in ideas, feelings and characters that the viewer freely gives way to the spell. *Maurice*…is such a film."

The frequently vitriolic (and often none-too-gay-friendly) John Simon wrote in *National Review* that *Maurice* was Merchant and Ivory's "best film to date." The movie, he said, has a "quality of rapture without ostentation…. This is a film with shape and psychological concerns, rare in today's cinema."

Critic Judith Crist called it "timeless and unforgettable...an exquisite film...."

The Village Voice's Stephen Harvey labeled it "a more remarkable achievement than *A Room With a View.*"

And *Newsweek*'s David Ansen applauded the film as "lovely," "languorous," and "ravishing."

Gay critic Vito Russo, best known as the author of *The Celluloid Closet,* reviewed the film for *The Nation. Maurice,* he said, was, "the first film to tell a gay love story in a casual, unselfconscious way. It demystifies homosexual love by establishing the universality of desire. It is also the first widely respected film to suggest that homosexuality ought not to be a controversial issue." He described the film itself as "lushly beautiful."

One of the few dissenting voices was Richard Schickel in *Time.* He complained that the film was "enervated...all high-mindedness and good taste. It has no emotional tension."

Epilogue: Maurice did respectable box office, and despite some fears that Merchant and Ivory had risked their careers by making the film, they went on to film *Howards End*—regarded by many critics as their crowning achievement—in 1992 and the superbly poignant *The Remains of the Day* the year after that.

7. ***The Adventures of Priscilla, Queen of the Desert* (1994)**

The film: First pitched as a musical about two drag queens and a transsexual driving a bus named Priscilla across the Australian outback, *Priscilla, Queen of the Desert* was initially intended to have original songs and a host of big-name stars in cameo roles. However, the idea of an original score was eventually dropped, as was the notion of filling the cast with high-priced stars. After that, one of the biggest problems facing producers was casting the central roles: specifically the part of Bernadette, the wise and world-weary transsexual whose struggle to find happiness is at the heart of the film. Among those who were approached were John Cleese (he refused) and Tony Curtis (after initially expressing enthusiasm, he stopped returning the producers' phone calls). Other actors who were considered included William Shatner, Colin Firth, Christopher Reeve, Peter O'Toole, Albert Finney, Alan Bates, and Tim

Curry. There was even a brief consideration of filling the part with a female star, such as Julie Andrews or Ann-Margret. The role finally went to British film veteran Terence Stamp, best known for his dashing performances in such films as *Far From the Madding Crowd* and *Modesty Blaise* in the 1960s. ("I couldn't believe it," he told an interviewer after *Priscilla* was finished. "I looked like some old hooker, you know. If I'd been a real girl, I'd have gone to bed in tears.") When the modestly budgeted film was finally premiered at the 1994 Cannes Film Festival, it elicited a standing ovation from the audience.

What the critics said: Most critics gently praised the film (with a special nod to its poignance), while singling out Stamp's extraordinary, Oscar-caliber performance for special recognition.

Leah Rozen, in *People,* called the film "fabulously excessive... often funny and occasionally touching."

Critic Guy Flatley, writing in *Cosmopolitan,* described *Priscilla* as "wacky and unexpectedly touching.... It's a bus well worth boarding."

Janet Maslin, in *The New York Times,* praised the film as "flamboyantly colorful, sweetly old-fashioned," while Kenneth Turan in the *Los Angeles Times* lauded its "comic pizazz" and "bawdy dazzle."

There were two conflicting opinions in *Entertainment Weekly.* Critic Lisa Schwarzbaum loved the film's "audacious humor and gaudy sumptuousness" and described Stamp's performance as "regal.... I didn't expect to be so moved." However, critic Lawrence O'Toole dismissed the film as "brash" and "self-patronizing." "The gay humor can be pedestrian," he wrote, "and the drag is often dreadful." But, he said, "Stamp is wonderfully subtle."

Bruce Williamson, in *Playboy,* gave it three "bunnies" (meaning "good show") and, while praising Stamp's performance in particular, he commended the film in general for its "outrageously entertaining jokes."

Epilogue: Priscilla was one of the undisputed "sleeper" hits of 1994.

However, one of the only people to publicly and outspokenly condemn the film was Nathan Sanders, editor of an Abba fanzine in the U.S. Specifically, he objected to a scene in the film in which Guy Pearce unveils his most precious Abba keepsake, a bit of fecal material in a bottle from singer Agnetha Faltskog. Sanders denounced the film as "disappointing and disgusting" and vowed to mount an international boycott against it. "This won't be the last you will hear from Abba fans on this matter," he warned the producers.

To the disappointment of many, Terence Stamp's performance, hailed by numerous critics as a shoo-in for the Oscars, was not even nominated. The film did, however, win an Academy Award for costume design.

66 Notable Actors Who Have Appeared in Drag in the Movies

1. Charlie Chaplin (*The Masquerader,* 1914; *A Woman,* 1915)
2. Lon Chaney (*The Unholy Three,* 1925)
3. Lionel Barrymore (*Devil Doll,* 1936)
4. Jack Benny (*Charley's Aunt,* 1941)
5. Mickey Rooney (*Babes on Broadway,* 1941)
6. William Powell (*Love Crazy,* 1941)
7. Lou Costello (*Lost in a Harem,* 1944)
8. Cary Grant (*I Was a Male War Bride,* 1949)
9. Alec Guinness (*Kind Hearts and Coronets,* 1949)
10. Ray Bolger (*Where's Charley,* 1952)
11. Robert Morse (*The Matchmaker,* 1958)
12. Anthony Perkins (*The Matchmaker,* 1958; *Psycho,* 1960)
13. Tony Curtis (*Some Like It Hot,* 1959)
14. Jack Lemmon (*Some Like It Hot,* 1959)
15. Peter Sellers (*The Mouse That Roared,* 1959)
16. Bing Crosby (*High Time,* 1960)
17. Danny Kaye (*On the Double,* 1961)
18. Edd Byrnes (*Beach Ball,* 1965)
19. Jack Gilford (*A Funny Thing Happened on the Way to the Forum,* 1966)

20. Phil Silvers (*A Funny Thing Happened on the Way to the Forum,* 1966)
21. Paul Lynde (*The Glass Bottom Boat,* 1966)
22. Lee J. Cobb (*In Like Flint,* 1967)
23. Dudley Moore (*Bedazzled,* 1967)
24. Ray Walston (*Caprice,* 1967)
25. Christopher Hewett (*The Producers,* 1968)
26. Helmut Berger (*The Damned,* 1969)
27. Yul Brynner (*The Magic Christian,* 1970)
28. George Sanders (*The Kremlin Letter,* 1970)
29. Joel Grey (*Cabaret,* 1972)
30. Lou Jacobi (*Everything You Always Wanted to Know About Sex, But Were Afraid to Ask,* 1972)
31. Jeff Bridges (*Thunderbolt and Lightfoot,* 1974)
32. Tim Curry (*The Rocky Horror Picture Show,* 1975)
33. Marlon Brando (*The Missouri Breaks,* 1976)
34. Roman Polanski (*The Tenant,* 1976)
35. Michel Serrault (*La Cage aux Folles,* 1978; *La Cage aux Folles II,* 1980; *La Cage aux Folles III,* 1986)
36. Michael Caine (*Dressed to Kill,* 1980)
37. Adam West (*The Happy Hooker Goes Hollywood,* 1980)
38. George Hamilton (*Zorro, The Gay Blade,* 1981)
39. Rutger Hauer (*Chanel Solitaire,* 1981)
40. Robert Vaughn (*S.O.B.*, 1981)
41. John Lithgow (*The World According to Garp,* 1982)
42. Steve Martin (*Dead Men Don't Wear Plaid,* 1982)
43. Robert Preston (*Victor/Victoria,* 1982)
44. Dustin Hoffman (*Tootsie,* 1983)
45. Ted McGinley (*Revenge of the Nerds,* 1984)
46. Gene Simmons (*Never Too Young To Die,* 1985)
47. John Candy (*Armed and Dangerous,* 1986; *Nothing But Trouble,* 1991)
48. Dom DeLuise (*Haunted Honeymoon,* 1986)
49. Gerard Depardieu (*Menage,* 1986)
50. Richard Pryor (*Jo Jo Dancer, Your Life Is Calling,* 1986)
51. Harvey Fierstein (*Torch Song Trilogy,* 1988)
52. Michael J. Fox (*Back to the Future II,* 1989)

53. Kurt Russell (*Tango & Cash,* 1989)
54. Kevin Bacon (*JFK,* 1991)
55. Dabney Coleman (*Meet the Applegates,* 1991)
56. Jaye Davidson (*The Crying Game,* 1992)
57. Hulk Hogan (*Mr. Nanny,* 1993)
58. John Lone (*M. Butterfly,* 1993)
59. Mr. T (*Freaked,* 1993)
60. Robin Williams (*Mrs. Doubtfire,* 1993)
61. Johnny Depp (*Ed Wood,* 1994)
62. John Hurt (*Even Cowgirls Get the Blues,* 1994)
63. Terence Stamp (*The Adventures of Priscilla, Queen of the Desert,* 1994)
64. John Leguizamo (*To Woo Fong, Thanks for Everything, Julie Newmar,* 1995)
65. Wesley Snipes (*To Woo Fong, Thanks for Everything, Julie Newmar,* 1995)
66. Patrick Swayze (*To Woo Fong, Thanks for Everything, Julie Newmar,* 1995)

2 Unfinished Gay Novels by Famous Writers

1. *The Novel of an Invert* by Emile Zola (c. 1885)

Zola's novels were frequently condemned as pornography by conservative readers, and he often did his best to fan the flames of controversy, partly because he enjoyed the attention and partly because controversy helped to boost sales of his books. His celebrated novel about prostitution, *Nana* (which included references to lesbianism), was denounced as "gutter-sweeping" by some readers, and another, *La Terre,* was prosecuted in court by a member of the British Parliament who believed "nothing more diabolical has ever been written by the pen of man." But even the great French writer, for all of his disdain of middle-class morality, was worried about writing a novel about homosexuality. In the 1880s, as part of his twenty-volume *Natural and Social History of a Family Under the Second Empire,* he started work on a novel called, simply, *The Novel of an Invert.* However, he finally abandoned it because he was afraid to publish it. His views on homosexuality sometimes seemed to contradict one another. He once wrote that "an invert is a disorganizer of family, of the nation, of humanity." On the other hand, he was also one of a handful of famous European literary figures who publicly backed Magnus Hirschfeld's international campaign to repeal stiffly antihomosexual laws in Germany around the turn of the century.

2. *Flowers of Asphalt* by Stephen Crane (1894)
Crane was already widely known for his novel about female prostitution, *Maggie,* when he decided, after being approached by a young male hustler in New York City, to write a novel about homosexuality, tentatively titled *Flowers of Asphalt.* On an April night in 1894, Crane and a friend had been walking down Broadway when they were approached by what they at first thought was a young beggar but who turned out to be a male prostitute soliciting them. Intrigued, Crane invited the boy home, fed him, listened to his stories, and then gave him fifty dollars. Almost immediately Crane started work on *Flowers of Asphalt,* about a boy who flees the country for New York City and becomes a prostitute. Parts of the manuscript were warmly praised by some of Crane's friends, but he apparently abandoned work on it after he read portions of it to author Hamlin Garland. Garland begged him to stop wasting his time and talent on such horrifying material. The unfinished manuscript has never been found.

3 Suppressed Manuscripts of Famous Gay Men

1. ***Maurice*** **by E.M. Forster**

The author of such English classics as *A Passage to India* and *A Room With a View* kept his most revealing manuscript under lock and key. *Maurice,* a novel about homosexual love, was begun by Forster in 1913, after an encounter with English social reformer Edward Carpenter and his lover, George Merrill. It was finished the following year. Forster believed that the novel's happy ending would prevent the book from being published in his lifetime. "If it ended unhappily," he wrote, "with a lad dangling from a noose or with a suicide pact, all would be well.... But the lovers get away unpunished and consequently recommend crime." After Forster's death in 1970, all of his unpublished works, including *Maurice,* went to King's College, Cambridge. *Maurice* was finally published in 1971.

2. The memoirs of Herman Bang

Bang was one of Denmark's leading nineteenth-century novelists and poets. After his death in 1912, there were rumors that he had left behind some memoir in which he posthumously revealed his homosexuality. Magnus Hirschfeld's Scientific Humanitarian Committee, an early gay rights group in Germany, urged the publication of the manuscript: "It is to be hoped that Herman Bang, who had an enthusiastic interest for our movement, spoke out even more clearly about the emotional side of his life in some manuscript that he may have left behind and that will hopefully not be withheld from the public." Unfortunately, Bang's literary executor and publisher, Peter Nansen, claimed that the work would bring "monstrous harm to Bang's name" and decided to suppress it.

3. The memoirs of John Addington Symonds

For eighteen months, from 1889 to 1890, English essayist and historian John Addington Symonds poured his energies into writing his memoirs, in which he candidly discussed his homosexuality and the personal torment of coming to terms with it. Symonds was anxious that the work be published—he thought it would be useful to later psychologists and researchers—but not until "a period when it will not be injurious to my family." When Symonds died in 1893, the work fell into the hands of his literary executor, Horatio Brown. When Brown died in 1926, he in turn bequeathed it to the London Library, with specific instructions that it not be published for fifty years. From 1926 to 1949, the work languished, unopened. The first person to ask permission to read it was Symonds's own daughter, Dame Katharine Furse, in 1949; but it wasn't until 1954 that the library finally provided public access to the memoirs, and even then, because of its subject matter, only to "bona fide scholars." It wasn't until 1984—almost one hundred years after it was written—that the manuscript was finally published.

The Top 10 All-time Best-selling Gay and Lesbian Titles at Lambda Rising Bookstore in Washington, D.C.

1. *The Front Runner* by Patricia Nell Warren
2. *A Boy's Own Story* by Edmund White
3. *Faggots* by Larry Kramer
4. *Tales of the City* by Armistead Maupin
5. *Becoming a Man* by Paul Monette
6. *Member of the Family* edited by John Preston
7. *The Best Little Boy in the World* by John Reid
8. *Invisible Life* by E. Lyn Harris
9. *Rubyfruit Jungle* by Rita Mae Brown
10. *Stone Butch Blues* by Leslie Feinberg

NOTE: Lambda Rising, one of the largest gay bookstores in the world, first opened its doors in the summer of 1974. At that time it stocked approximately three hundred titles and averaged sales of $25 a day. Today, it offers more than twenty thousand titles and has annual sales over $1.5 million.

5 "Dirty" Gay Novels Written Before 1930

1. *The Sins of the Cities of the Plain; or the Recollections of a Mary-Anne* (1881)

Written more than a decade before Oscar Wilde was sentenced to prison for lewd conduct with various young men and street hustlers, *The Sins of the Cities of the Plain* recounts the adventures of a successful male prostitute, Jack Saul, working the streets of late-nineteenth-century London. Based on fact, it revealed a widespread, steamy side of Victorian society and includes, among other episodes, the explicit confessions of a young soldier in the Foot Guards—"There are lots of houses in London where only soldiers are received and where gentlemen can sleep with them"—and a description of a transvestite ball at a fashionable London hotel. "I believe the people of the house thought we were gay ladies," one of the characters remarks after leaving the ball. The book concludes that "the extent to which pederasty is carried on in London between gentlemen and young fellows is little dreamed of by the outside public." Although it was less than a hundred pages long and expensively priced at four guineas a volume, the book sold very well.

2. *Teleny, or the Reverse of the Medal: A Physiological Romance of Today* (1893)

Often attributed to Oscar Wilde, who probably only helped edit it, *Teleny* describes a passionate and tragic love affair between two men: the handsome young pianist Rene Teleny and one of his adoring fans, Camille Des Grieux. Considered the most prominent example of nineteenth-century gay erotica, the book is florid in style and operatic in tone: People scream for mercy during sex and faint in the throes of orgasm, and, more often than not, an aroused penis is described in terms more appropriate to the launching of a battleship. It's the kind of book where people are not merely charismatic but, rather, "diabolically charismatic." Almost every sexual encounter, gay or straight, has an unhappy outcome: A young maid kills herself after a sexual affair with a man; a handsome Arab has a bottle accidentally broken up his rectum during an orgy; and Des Grieux himself makes two unsuccessful suicide attempts, largely because he cannot cope with his "unnatural" desires. Perhaps fittingly, in the book's final, lurid chapter, Teleny himself commits suicide after he prostitutes himself for some badly needed cash to Des Grieux's beautiful and wealthy mother.

3. ***Pederastie Active*** **(1906)**
The author of this short French classic identified himself to history only as Mr. P. D. Rast. Written in a lighthearted, often farcical style, the book tells the story of an older man who seduces one willing male virgin after another. "A virgin boy's jissom is incomparably delicious," the author explains. "Only you who have tasted it, you blessed mortals, can know it!" His list of conquests includes two beautiful young brothers, Albert and Philippe, who he enjoys together in one sitting, and a handsome soldier named Thomas. Describing his fling in bed with Thomas, the author muses, in a style typical of the entire narrative, "God! Was he lovable! Especially his huge plunger. Ah, reader, pity my poor little asshole, because this terrifying machine is going to burrow itself so deeply that its blond fur will caress my orifice!"

4. ***Ernest*** **(1910)**
Privately published in a limited edition by its author, the German book collector Werner von Bleichroeder, *Ernest* is the story of a beautiful nephew sexually enslaved by his strong, good-looking uncle, Gernand. "You are going to get used to the idea that your nudity and every part of your body belong to me," Gernand tells

the boy, "and perhaps to quite a few other people besides, if I so choose." Young Ernest—who is devoted to his muscular uncle—is subjected to mouth fuckings, fierce spankings, piss baths, and lessons in masturbation and fellatio and is admonished that he is to become the willing sexual plaything of his classmates at school or of any man who wants him. "These are the first lessons in the art of satisfying a man with your mouth," Gernand explains to the boy. "That will be henceforth your main job.... Your face and mouth are made for it, and countless members will come to enjoy themselves in your little mouth, big ones and small ones, young ones and old ones, fat ones and skinny ones. And you will suck them all, till the hot stream of their passion is appeased by pouring down your throat!" In the final pages of the book, Ernest is forced into prostitution at a bar belonging to a well-hung ex-sailor, a friend of Gernand.

5. *The White Paper* (1928)

"I have always loved the stronger sex," remarks the narrator of *The White Paper* at the start of the book. "As long as I can remember, and even looking back to that age when the senses have still to come under the influence of the mind, I find traces of the love I have always had for boys." Usually attributed to Jean Cocteau, *The White Paper* describes an adolescent boy's growing passion for classmates, sailors, and other working-class boys in the French port city of Toulon. Although the book contained a preface and several erotic illustrations by Cocteau, he never publicly acknowledged its authorship; however, it is widely regarded as "the most signatured of unsigned works." In one of the book's most memorable early episodes, the narrator develops a blinding crush on a virile, well-developed classmate at school; trying to declare his love to the boy, he makes a complete fool of himself instead. The boy, who charms everyone around him, later dies of pneumonia after an ill-advised swim in the Seine. In another scene the narrator goes to a public bath where the proprietor has installed transparent mirrors so that he and his friends can watch men bathing: "Young members of the working class provided the show.... Standing in the tub, they would gaze at their reflection (at me) pensively and start with a

Parisian grin which exposes the gums. Next, they'd scratch a shoulder, pick up the soap, and, handling it slowly, make it bubble into a lather. Then they'd soap themselves. The soaping would gradually turn into caressing. All of a sudden their eyes would wander out of this world, their heads would tilt back, and their bodies would spit like furious animals." The book ends with the narrator—wounded by the world's lack of acceptance of his sexuality—exiling himself from society.

12 Books Recently Banned, or Nearly Banned, Because of Gay and Lesbian Themes

1. ***The Celluloid Closet: Homosexuality in the Movies* by Vito Russo**

In 1993, citizens of Bend, Oregon, tried to have it removed from the shelves of the county library because it "encourages and condones" homosexuality.

2. ***Is It a Choice? Answers to Three Hundred of the Most Frequently Asked Questions About Gays and Lesbians* by Eric Marcus**

Attempts to ban it in 1993 from the Indianola, Iowa, public library were based on the claim it was not "of much concern to the Christian-believing people of this community." Three years earlier an attempt had been made to ban another of Marcus's books, *The Male Couple's Guide to Living Together,* from the Muscatine, Iowa, public library, on the grounds it was "immoral."

3. ***The Claiming of Sleeping Beauty* by Anne Rice**

In 1992, Rice's "Beauty" series (written under the pseudonym A.E. Roquelaire) was banned from the Lake Lanier regional library system in Georgia.

4. ***The Color Purple* by Alice Walker**

Walker's acclaimed novel had a long history of being banned, especially from high school libraries, during the 1980s. That trend continued in 1992, when it was banned from—and labeled as "smut" by—the Souderton, Pennsylvania, area school district. There were also unsuccessful attempts, in 1990 and 1992, to have it banned from school libraries in Wyoming and North Carolina.

5. ***The New Joy of Gay Sex* by Dr. Charles Silverstein and Felice Picano**

In 1994, seven hundred patrons of the River Bluffs regional library in St. Joseph, Missouri, submitted a petition condemning it as "pornography" and demanding, unsuccessfully, that it be removed from the library's shelves. A year earlier there had been an unsuccessful attempt to have it banned from the public library in Helena, Montana.

6. ***Boys and Sex* by Wardell Pomeroy**

It was banned in 1990 from a middle school library in Black River Falls, Wisconsin, in part because it dealt with homosexuality and masturbation. Four years later it was banned from a school library in Rangely, Colorado, for the same reasons.

7. ***Human Sexuality* by Elizabeth Winship, et al.**

Claiming that it "didn't stress abstinence from sex" and that "it didn't say whether sexual relations before marriage, homosexuality, masturbation, or abortion are right or wrong," parents in the Belleville, Missouri, school district had the textbook removed from use in classes in 1994. That same year it was also banned from high schools in Fulton County, Georgia, after parents complained that the book did not do enough to discourage students from engaging in sex.

8. ***Daddy's Roommate* by Michael Willhoite**

Since 1990, attempts have been made to ban it from more than twenty public libraries in Washington, Wisconsin, Oregon, North Carolina, New Mexico, Georgia, Florida, Massachusetts, New Jersey, Tennessee, and numerous other states. An attempt to have it removed from the Mesa, Arizona, public library was based on the assertion that it "is vile and it goes against every law and constitution." In at least a half dozen cities' public libraries, it has been moved from the children's section to the adult section.

9. *Understanding Your Sexual Identity: A Book for Gay Teens & Their Friends* by Janice Rench
In 1994 it was banned from the library shelves of the Rangely, Colorado, middle school. That same year it was also removed from the shelves of a middle school library in Washington Township, New Jersey.

10. *Annie on My Mind* by Nancy Garden
In 1993 and 1994 it was banned from a number of high school libraries in Missouri and Kansas because of its lesbian subject matter. In 1994, Christian protesters in Kansas City, Missouri, publicly burned copies of the book.

11. *I Once Had a Master* by John Preston
Canadian customs officials seized copies of it as well as Preston's *Entertainment for a Master* in 1992 on the grounds that it was obscene and promoted sadomasochism. The books were part of a shipment of gay titles to the Little Sisters Book and Art Emporium in Vancouver, which has, through the years, suffered numerous seizures of gay-themed shipments by customs authorities.

12. *Macho Sluts* by Pat Califia
In 1989 the book was banned by Canadian customs authorities, in part because of its graphic portrayals of sadomasochistic sex and anal penetration. The ban was rescinded six months later. In 1992 it was once again banned by Canadian officials, and once again the ban was later lifted. The book has been banned (and then later ruled admissible) a total of five times in Canada. Other books that have recently been banned by Canadian authorities include: David Leavitt's *A Place I've Never Been,* Oscar Wilde's *Teleny,* Richard Mohr's *Gay Ideas,* David Wojnarowicz's *Memories That Smell Like Gasoline,* and Dorothy Alison's *Trash* as well as biographies of Cole Porter, Noël Coward, and Michelangelo. In their antigay zealotry,

customs officials have also, temporarily, banned such books as *Hot Hotter Hottest* (it turned out to be a chili pepper cookbook) and *Strokes* (which turned out to be a book on rowing).

...AND 1 BOOK THAT WAS BANNED BECAUSE IT DEALT WITH AIDS

1. ***What You Can Do to Avoid AIDS*** **by Magic Johnson**
In 1992, Kmart announced it was banning the book from its stores because of "the family orientation of Kmart customers" and because it was inappropriate in a store "where children shop." The Walgreen's drug store chain also announced it would ban the book due to its candid discussions of sexuality.

FROM SAPPHO TO MAPPLETHORPE: 19 OUTRAGEOUS ACTS OF CENSORSHIP IN THE HISTORY OF GAY PEOPLE

"Censorship of anything, at any time,
in any place, on whatever pretense,
has always been and always will be
the last cowardly resort of the boob and the bigot."
—*Eugene O'Neill*

1. Sappho's love poems
The greatest love poet of the ancient world, Sappho (610-580 B.C.) wrote hundreds of poems celebrating both homosexual and heterosexual love and was esteemed by the ancient Greeks as the "Tenth Muse." Unfortunately, several hundred years later Christian zealots did not agree. In A.D. 380 her books were ordered burned

by St. Gregory of Nazianzus, who dismissed her as "a lewd nymphomaniac." In 1073 what little of her work survived was subjected to another purge by decree of Pope Gregory VII: Sappho's poetry was publicly burned by ecclesiastical authorities in both Constantinople and Rome. By the twelfth century all that remained of Sappho's writing were two complete poems and a handful of fragments. In 1897 archaeologists working in Egypt discovered numerous ancient coffins lined with papier-mâché scraps of papyrus scrolls, which turned out to be shredded fragments of Sappho's poetry. Similar scraps were also found wadded into the carcasses of mummified crocodiles and other animals at the same site. It is only because of this discovery that we have as much of her work as we do today, still only a scant five percent of the original body of her writing—seven hundred lines out of the estimated twelve thousand that she actually penned.

2. Male nudes in the Sistine Chapel

The powerful male nudes of Michelangelo's *The Last Judgment* scandalized much of Counter-Reformation Italy, and even the gay poet and pornographer Pietro Aretino expressed horror at the sight of so much nudity in the Sistine Chapel, the Pope's private place of worship. In 1559, five years before Michelangelo's death, the Vatican hired artist Daniele de Volterra to paint loincloths on the more explicit male nudes in the fresco, forever earning Volterra the mocking title il Brachettone—"the Breeches Maker." After the Council of Trent's rigid decrees on decency in 1563, *The Last Judgment* was actually threatened with complete destruction for a time. Only the protests of various Italian artists and noblemen saved the fresco from being completely whitewashed by zealous moralists.

3. Michelangelo's love sonnets

Michelangelo's genius was expressed not only as a painter and sculptor but also as a poet, and in 1623, fifty-nine years after his death, a volume of his impassioned love sonnets, most of them originally addressed to men, was published for the first time. Because of the explicitly homoerotic nature of many of the poems, the editor of the volume, Michelangelo's great-nephew, changed masculine pronouns to the feminine, deleted many of the more graphic homosexual references, and then bogusly claimed that all of the poems had actually been inspired by Vittoria Colonna, a devoutly religious sixty-year-old widow with whom Michelangelo had enjoyed a close friendship. It was not until almost 350 years later, in 1960, that a completely restored, definitive edition of the poems was finally published.

4. ***The Well of Loneliness***

A hysterical review in a London Sunday newspaper prompted English authorities to ban Radclyffe Hall's novel about lesbianism shortly after the book's publication in 1928. Critic James Douglas had written that he "would rather give a healthy boy or a healthy girl a phial of prussic acid than this novel"—a remark that immediately boosted the book's sales and sent vice authorities running to sweep up copies of it. At a public trial to decide whether or not the book was obscene, defense attorneys were forbidden from calling any of the forty literary critics they had assembled to testify on behalf of the novel. The presiding magistrate eventually ruled that the novel's literary merits—and he admitted it had many—actually worked against it, since the better written an immoral book was, the more corrupting was its influence. The book was judged obscene, and despite various appeals, not until twenty years later could it finally be published and sold in England.

Meanwhile, in the United States vice officers raided the office of the book's American publisher in 1929 and seized over eight hundred copies remaining from the sixth edition; they then staged a similar raid on Macy's book department. New York publisher Donald S. Friede was arrested and charged with circulating indecent literature. Like their English counterparts, American attorneys sought to defend the book on the grounds that it had literary merit; however, as in England, the court ruled that the testimony of literary experts was inadmissible. Despite the fact that the novel had been praised by Havelock Ellis, George Bernard Shaw, H.G. Wells, and others, the U.S. court finally ruled that "the book can have no moral value since it seeks to justify the right of a pervert to prey upon normal members of a community...." The judge further declared that although the book contained no obscene words or indecent phrases, its subject matter was "calculated to corrupt and debase." He ordered that it be banned. A few months later, however, a higher court overturned his decision, and *The Well of Loneliness* was finally cleared for sale in the U.S. Thanks in large part to all of the accusations of obscenity surrounding it, the novel eventually sold in excess of 100,000 copies.

5. ***The Life of Horatio Alger***
American writer Horatio Alger (1834-1899) was best known for his "rags to riches" boys' novels, which were popular in the late nineteenth century. Alger himself was ardently homosexual, with a penchant for teenage boys; he was once run out of Brewster, Massachusetts, for his sexual involvement with some of the local youths. Herbert Mayes's "definitive" biography of Alger, published in 1928, made no mention of Alger's homosexuality but instead portrayed him as a fun-loving heterosexual with a taste for fast women. Mayes's biography was the standard reference work on Alger's life for over sixty years. However, in 1974 Mayes confessed that the entire biography had been a fabrication, that he had completely censored the true facts of Alger's life and had invented the existence of a Horatio Alger diary that the biography was supposedly based on.

6. ***The Last Judgment,* again**
In 1933, Michelangelo's Sistine Chapel nudes were once again the center of controversy. In New York City, U.S. customs agents seized and held a shipment of European art books containing reproductions of Michelangelo's *The Last Judgment.* An assistant collector of customs, who had never heard of Michelangelo, deemed the reproductions obscene. A few days later a very embarrassed Treasury Department acknowledged the mistake and relinquished the books.

7. The 1936 film version of *The Children's Hour*
In 1936, Lillian Hellman's play about lesbianism, *The Children's Hour,* was brought to the screen by producer Samuel Goldwyn and director William Wyler. Retitled *These Three,* the play was substan-

tially bowdlerized: All of its lesbian characters were changed to heterosexuals, and the central lesbian love interest was changed to a standard heterosexual love triangle. By authority of the Motion Picture Production Code (whose job it was to safeguard public morals), censors forbade the studio and even film critics from mentioning that the movie had been based on Hellman's play.

8. The works of André Gide

In 1935 a New York bookseller was arrested and charged with circulating indecent literature after he sold a copy of Gide's autobiography, *If It Die,* to an undercover police officer. The book recounted Gide's coming to terms with his homosexuality as a young man. Fortunately, Judge Nathan D. Perlman later ruled that although Gide had "unveiled the darker corners of his life," the autobiography "as a complete entity was not obscene." In 1952, five years after Gide had won the Nobel Prize for literature, all of his works were placed on the Catholic Index of Forbidden Books. They were considered dangerous to faith and morals. Ironically, all of his works had also recently been banned in the Soviet Union.

9. *The New York Times* and Gore Vidal

When Gore Vidal's novel *The City and the Pillar* was published in 1948, *The New York Times* not only refused to run ads for it, because of the book's theme, male homosexuality, but also refused to review it. The *Times'* daily reviewer, Orville Prescott, disgustedly announced he would never review a book by Vidal again. It wasn't until sixteen years later, with the publication of *Julian,* that the *Times* relented and reviewed one of Vidal's novels. "As we all know," Vidal later remarked wryly, "I invented homosexuality in 1948 with *The City and the Pillar.*"

10. *A Streetcar Named Desire*

In Tennessee Williams's play, Blanche du Bois's young husband—a boy who shot himself on the beach one night—was a homosexual. For the 1951 screen version, the Motion Picture Production Code dictated that the homosexuality be entirely eliminated: In the film Blanche's husband suffers merely from "nervousness." The film's director, Elia Kazan, said,

"I wouldn't put the homosexuality back in the picture if the code had been revised last night and it was now permissible. I don't want it. I prefer debility and weakness over any kind of suggestion of perversion."

11. **Allen Ginsberg's poetry**
In 1957 two officers of the San Francisco police department arrested poet and publisher Lawrence Ferlinghetti on charges of having published *Howl and Other Poems* by gay poet Allen Ginsberg. Police captain William Hanrahan described the work as "obscene and filthy," and told reporters, "When I say 'filthy,' I don't mean *suggestive.* I mean *filthy words that are vulgar.*" After a lengthy trial and two weeks of deliberation, Judge Clayton Horn freed Ferlinghetti and ruled that Ginsberg's poetry was not obscene. Horn's written opinion, which is still regarded as a major codification of the obscenity law in California, pointed out: "Life is not encased in one formula whereby everyone acts the same or conforms to a particular pattern. No two persons think alike. We are all made from the same mould, but in different patterns. Would there be any freedom of press or speech if one must reduce his vocabulary to vapid innocuous euphemism? An author should be…allowed to express his thoughts and ideas in his own words."

12. **The *H* words**
In 1961 the Motion Picture Association of America relaxed its thirty-year code prohibiting the portrayal of homosexuality on America's movie screens. However, in 1962 the MPAA still refused to grant its Seal of Approval to Basil Dearden's film *Victim,* because it actually used the words "homosexual" and "homosexuality" on-screen.

13. **Gay personals ads**
In 1969 a well-known London underground newspaper, the *International Times,* began running personals ads for gay men alongside its usual personals for heterosexuals. The new section was called, simply, "Males." Police subsequently raided the newspaper's editorial offices and the paper's printers. The newspaper's three directors were charged with conspiring "to induce readers to resort to… homosexual practices and thereby to debauch and corrupt public

morals." They were also charged with conspiring "to outrage public decency by inserting advertisements containing lewd, disgusting and offensive matter." All three men were found guilty. The House of Lords was asked to review the case and decided, by a 4-1 majority, that the newspaper's directors had been rightfully convicted of conspiring to corrupt public morals. But, perplexingly, they set aside the conviction for conspiring to outrage public decency—leading one wry commentator to note that what corrupts us does not apparently outrage us.

14. Newspaper ads for *The Boys in the Band*

When William Friedkin's film version of *The Boys in the Band* opened across the country in 1970, major daily newspapers in Chicago, San Francisco, and Boston refused at first to carry ads for it. The ads showed actor Leonard Frey on the left side of the ad with the caption TODAY IS HAROLD'S BIRTHDAY; on the right side was a picture of actor Robert La Tourneaux, portraying a hustler, with the caption THIS IS HIS PRESENT. Ads for the R-rated movie were also initially rejected by the *Los Angeles Times* and the New York *Daily News.*

15. *Cabaret* on prime time

When ABC first broadcast Bob Fosse's *Cabaret* on prime time in 1975, all references to homosexuality and bisexuality, including the crucial plot element of Brian's affair with Maximilian, were removed by network censors.

16. A poem about Christ

The editor and publishers of London's *Gay News* were put on trial in 1977 for having published a poem—"The Love That Dares to Speak Its Name" by noted scholar-translator James Kirkup—in which a Roman centurion removes the body of Christ from the cross and performs an act of fellatio on it. The paper was charged under a little-known—and little-used—blasphemous libel law, which made it a crime to ridicule or impugn Jesus Christ or any part of the Holy Scriptures. During the trial the prosecution repeatedly linked all homosexual acts to child molestation and portrayed the *Gay News* as a biweekly manifesto for pedophiliacs. After the judge in the case disallowed any defense of the poem or the newspaper on literary or theological grounds, a guilty verdict became a foregone conclusion, and *Gay News* editor Denis Lemon became the planet's only living convicted blasphemer.

17. Robert Mapplethorpe's photographs

In 1989 the Corcoran Gallery of Art in Washington, D.C., acting under intense pressure from powerful Washington conservatives, canceled a scheduled exhibit of photographs by renowned gay photographer Robert Mapplethorpe. The exhibit, titled "The Perfect Moment," included Mapplethorpe's famous studies of flowers and nudes as well as photographs of gay sadomasochistic sex acts and a photograph of a little girl exposing her genitals. "It was a close call," the gallery's chairman told the press. "If you went ahead, I suppose you could say you were upholding freedom of artistic expression against possible political pressure." The gallery's decision ignited a national controversy over Mapplethorpe's work and over the National Endowment of the Arts, which had partly financed the exhibit. In the face of widespread criticism within the artistic community, the Corcoran eventually issued a public apology for the cancellation—and the gallery's director, Christina Orr-Cahall, resigned—but its reputation was still seriously damaged. In a belated attempt to salvage its name, it hastily announced plans to present an exhibit on the history of censorship. Meanwhile, the Mapplethorpe exhibit had moved on to the Contemporary Arts Center in Cincinnati, despite vows by that city's officials to close the show if it opened. "The people of this community do not cater to what others depict as art," Cincinnati's police chief told reporters. He promised to seize any photographs in the exhibit that were obscene. On April 7, 1990, after the exhibit had opened, police raided the Arts Center, forced all visitors to leave, and began videotaping Mapplethorpe's photographs as evidence. The center's director, Dennis Barrie, was arrested and charged with obscenity and misuse of a minor in pornography. Six months later both Barrie and the Arts Center were acquitted of all charges. "I'm not an expert," said one juror in the case. "I don't understand Picasso's art, but I assume the people who call it art know what they're talking about."

18. **A study on teenage suicide**
A 1989 U.S. government study on gay teen suicide was banned from public release by the Bush administration's secretary of Health and Human Services, Louis Sullivan, on the grounds that the report's statistical conclusions "undermine the institution of the family." The study had found that a third of all teen suicides in the U.S. are by gay and lesbian youths and that suicide is the leading cause of death among gay and lesbian teenagers. The suppressed study had been part of a broader report on the national epidemic of teenage suicide.

19. **"We Are the Champions"**
In 1992 eighth-graders at Sacred Heart School in Clifton, New Jersey, were forbidden from playing the song "We Are the Champions," by the British rock group Queen, at their graduation ceremonies. School officials refused to allow the song after learning that Queen's lead singer, Freddie Mercury, was gay and had died of AIDS complications a year earlier. When students tried to protest the decision, officials canceled the entire graduation ceremony rather than let the song be played.

26 Classic Gay Graffiti

1. Don't accept candy from strangers—get real estate.

2. "My mother made me a homosexual."
"If I send her some yarn, will she make me one too?"

3. Edith Head gives great costume.

4. If homosexuality is an illness,
we should all call in "queer" to work tomorrow.

5. "I am twelve inches long and three inches around."
"Great, how big is your cock?"

6. Practice makes pervert.

7. Here I sit my heart a bustin',
Sucked four cocks and still a lustin'.

8. Here I sit alone and confused,
Tried to hustle but was only cruised.

9. Men are like floor tiles—if you lay them right the first time, you can walk all over them forever.

10. Old fairies never die, they just blow away.

11. FCK—the only thing missing is you.

12. The big difference between my lover and my job is that after five years my job still sucks.

13. My lover has had crabs so many times, he qualifies as an aquarium.

14. Fight heterosexual supremacy—fuck a straight man today!

15. An ill Finn blows no good.

16. The Pope decided to exonerate the Jews for the crucifixion; he's going to blame it on the queers instead.

17. Beat me,
Whip me,
Use me,
Fuck me—
But if you mess up my hair, *you die!*

18. Young man, well-hung, with beautiful body,
is willing to do anything.
P.S. Bill, if you see this, don't bother to call—
it's only me, Tony.

19. Men that I can't get are men that I ain't met.

20. "Edith Sitwell is a transvestite."
"She's dead, you dope."
"OK, Edith Sitwell is a dead transvestite."

21. I peek while they're pissing,
I watch while they shower,
Don't want to be missing,
A big cock in flower.
I'd like to be kissing
One this very hour.

22. Are you going to come quietly, or do I have to use earplugs?

23. There once was a boy named Bill
Who used a dynamite stick for a thrill.
They found his balls
Near Niagara Falls
And the head of his dick in Brazil.

24. Better latent than never.

25. Getting fucked when you have hemorrhoids
is like giving birth to a set of broken china.

26. "Peter had a bigger cock than Jesus."
"Yes, but Jesus has been screwing us for two thousand years."

15 Terrible Historical Events That Gay People Have Been Blamed For

1. The destruction of Sodom and Gomorrah
2. The fall of the Roman Empire
3. Plague in Constantinople (A.D. 543)
4. The fall of Visigothic Spain to the Muslims
5. The decline of medieval Arabic civilization
6. The Black Plague
7. The decline of Renaissance Italy
8. The poleworm infestation of the Netherlands (1730-1731)
9. The 1755 Lisbon earthquake
10. The rise of Nazi Germany
11. The assassination of President Kennedy
12. Earthquakes in California
13. The mid-1970s drought in the western U.S.
14. The appearance of AIDS
15. Hurricane Andrew

6 Early Christians Who Helped Shape the Church's Attitude Toward Homosexuals

"Virginity can be lost even by a thought."

—*St. Jerome*

1. Philo Judaeus (20 B.C.-A.D. 50), Alexandrian philosopher

 Philo claimed that homosexuality was on the increase in his own time, that homosexual practices led to sterility, and that homosexual men seduced and corrupted heterosexual men in order to spread "the disease of effemination." Male homosexuality, he believed, should be punished by death. His writings strongly influenced the development of early Christian ideology. For example, Philo was among the first Christians to expressly interpret the story of the destruction of Sodom and Gomorrah in homosexual terms. (Actually, the people of Sodom were probably destroyed for the sins of pride, adultery, and inhospitality; the Bible makes no mention of homosexuality in connection with the story.) In other matters: Philo regarded the body as a prison and approved of circumcision because he thought it blunted a man's pleasure in intercourse. He often railed against women, since they were, in his opinion, the cause of man's fall in the Garden of Eden.

2. Clement of Alexandria (150-215), early Christian teacher and apologist

Born of non-Christian parents in Athens, Clement was converted to Christianity in his twenties while still a student. He has been called "one of the major intellectual leaders" of early Christianity. In his ethical and theological works, he condemned homosexuality, along with masturbation, oral sex, anal sex, and sexual pleasure for its own sake. Homosexuals, he preached, "stand self-condemned by their fine robe, their sandals, their bearing, their way of walking, the cut of their hair, and their glances." He approved of laws condemning them to the mines. He believed that semen was a human being in its most primal form and that to expend it in anything but procreational coitus was tantamount to murder.

3. St. John Chrysostom (347-407), Archbishop of Constantinople

He called homosexuality "the most severe of all plagues…a new and insufferable crime" and preached that homosexual acts were worse than murder. He urged parents not to let their sons wear long hair: Long hair, he believed, was a sign of a corrupt spirit and made a boy more attractive to older men. Despite his horror of male homosexuality, he didn't think much of the alternative: He characterized women as "a necessary evil, a natural temptation, a desirable calamity, a domestic peril, a deadly fascination, a painted ill." He also wrote that lesbians were worse than male homosexuals, since women "ought to have more modesty." He condemned dancing, because it excited the emotions, and he denounced the theater, because he thought it taught people profanity, seduction, and intrigue. He is revered as one of the greatest teachers of the early Christian church.

4. St. Augustine (354-430), **Christian teacher and writer**
Augustine apparently had at least one homosexual affair in his youth, and he was, by his own admission, tormented throughout much of his early life by an "insatiable" desire for sex. He converted to Christianity when he was thirty-three, after he read Paul's epistles. After that he took a vow of celibacy and concluded that the Church had every right to coerce people into unity with Christ. He preached that all nonprocreational forms of sexuality—especially homosexuality—were grave sins and that even procreational sex between husband and wife was inherently shameful, because it involved lust and continued the cycle of man's guilt that had begun with Adam and Eve. Celibacy, he preached, was the most blessed state: The world, he said, would be improved if all reproduction should cease.

5. Justinian (483-565), **Byzantine emperor**
He made homosexual acts punishable by torture, mutilation, and death. Punishment sometimes included amputation of the hands, if sacrilege had also been committed, but usually took the form of castration, in most cases involving amputation of both the penis and the testicles. Justinian and his wife, Theodora, a former prostitute who continued her legendary sexual activities under a guise of Christian piety, freely used the charge of homosexuality against personal and political enemies. In one instance, when a young man publicly insulted Theodora, she accused him of being a homosexual: She had him brutally tortured and then had his penis lopped off so that he would bleed to death. Justinian blamed recent earthquakes, famine, and pestilence on homosexuals, who he claimed had provoked God's wrath.

6. St. Peter Damian (1007-1072), Christian reform leader
Orphaned at an early age and then brutalized by the older brother who raised him, Damian was tormented by sexual desire throughout his adolescence. To purge himself of carnal thoughts, he would immerse himself in ice water until his limbs were frozen and numb. As an adult he ranted against the prevalence of homosexuality among the clergy and begged the pope to take action against it. He characterized homosexuality as "the death of the body, the destruction of the soul" and claimed that even bestiality was preferable, since homosexuality involved the damnation of two souls, bestiality only one. He described the human body as "dirt" and "filth" and once wrote that a woman's labor pains were her just punishment for having engaged in intercourse.

Heavenly Fathers: 6 Gay or Bisexual Popes

1. Pope John XII (937-964)
An insatiable bisexual, he was accused of running a brothel out of St. Peter's. He used the papal treasury to pay off his gambling debts and enjoyed pranks such as ordaining a ten-year-old boy as bishop. Deposed once, he restored himself by force. He died in his late twenties, after being badly beaten by a jealous husband.

2. Pope Benedict IX (1020-1055)
Benedict turned the Lateran Palace into the site of lavish homosexual orgies, and by the time he was twenty-three, his riotous conduct was so appalling that he was deposed. He was reinstated and deposed several times over the next five years. After finally being driven out once and for all in 1048, he died in obscurity. Some Catholic records, perhaps self-servingly, portray him as having died as a penitent in a monastery.

3. **Pope Paul II** (1417-1471)
He wore a papal tiara that, according to one source, "outweighed a palace in its worth," and he plundered the papal treasury to satisfy his love of glitter and finery. Known to his cardinals as "Our Lady of Pity" for his tendency to cry at the slightest provocation, he allegedly died of a heart attack while being sodomized by one of his favorite boys.

4. **Pope Sixtus IV** (1414-1484)
He took one of his beautiful young nephews, Pietro Riario, as his lover. Riario was charming and witty, and Sixtus made him a millionaire by plundering the papal treasury. Another young nephew, Girolamo, was also alleged to have been Sixtus's lover. When Sixtus died, he left several million dollars in debts; but he is perhaps best remembered for consenting to the establishment of the Spanish Inquisition and for his appointment of Torquemada as its inquisitor-general.

5. **Pope Leo X** (1475-1521)
He acquired a reputation for being wildly extravagant. Among other things, he would play cards with his cardinals, allow the public to sit in as spectators, and toss huge handfuls of gold coins to the crowd whenever he won a hand. His expenses for both cultural and military endeavors, along with his taste for increasingly ornate papal gowns, drove the papal treasury into bankruptcy.

6. **Pope Julius III** (1487-1555)
He was lovers with both his bastard son, Bertuccino, and his adopted son, Innocente, and made both of them cardinals. He also appointed numerous other handsome teenage boys as cardinals and allegedly enjoyed bringing them together for orgies where he would watch them sodomize one another. Della Casa's famous poem "In Praise of Sodomy" was dedicated to him.

17 Gay-Porn Stars Who Died of AIDS Complications

1. Al Parker
2. J.W. King
3. John Holmes (a.k.a. "Johnny Wad")
4. Val Martin
5. Tony Bravo
6. Dave Connors
7. Mike Davis
8. Johnny Dawes
9. Kurt Marshall
10. Ed Dinakos
11. Casey Donovan
12. Bill Harrison
13. Beau Mathews
14. Jim Moore
15. Nick Rogers
16. Bob Shane
17. Ken J. Savoie

11 Famous People Who Lied About Having AIDS

1. Rudolf Nureyev (1938-1993), Russian dancer
Nureyev was diagnosed as being HIV-positive in 1984 but didn't manifest serious symptoms of the disease until 1991. Even as his condition worsened and he was forced to make public appearances in a wheelchair, he lied about his condition and suggested to reporters and colleagues that he was suffering from severe cardiac problems. When he died in Paris in 1993, a spokesman reported the cause of death as "a cardiac complication following a grievous illness." It was only a week later that Nureyev's longtime personal physician finally came forward with the truth. "If I clarify things now," said Dr. Michel Canesi, "it is because there is no such thing as a shameful disease. I am thinking of all the anonymous patients who are suffering from being ostracized. Rudolf lived for thirteen or fourteen years with this virus, thanks to his force, his combativeness. People should know that." Canesi explained that Nureyev

had hidden the truth about his HIV status for nearly a decade not out of vanity or embarrassment but out of fear that certain countries, especially the United States, would deny him entry if the truth were ever known.

2. Shaun McGill (1961-1992), Canadian figure skater

McGill—Canada's 1988 world professional silver medalist—kept his medical condition a secret for fear of being barred entry into the United States, where he often performed and worked as a choreographer and coach. Just a year before his death, he was stopped by U.S. immigration officials in Toronto who took him into a private room and interrogated him about his HIV status. McGill managed to convince them he had cancer, but only after he summoned a corroborating witness to vouch for him. (The witness was a friend who knew in advance to lie.) After McGill's death, the *Calgary Herald* revealed that more than forty top male figure skaters and coaches from the United States and Canada had died of AIDS complications. Like McGill, many of them felt compelled to lie about their medical condition in order to continue working in the U.S.

3. Rock Hudson (1925-1985), U.S. actor

After being diagnosed with AIDS in the summer of 1984, he lied about his condition to everyone except a handful of his closest friends. When acquaintances commented on his weight loss, he cheerfully told them he'd been exercising more. When colleagues commented on his pallor or lack of stamina, they were told he had had the flu and a couple of sleepless nights. Hudson's most intimate friends perpetuated the lie: Anyone who queried about his condition was taken aside and told, in the most confidential tones, that the actor was secretly suffering from anorexia and would soon be flying to a clinic in Switzerland for treatment. After Hudson collapsed in Paris in the summer of 1985 and was rushed to the American Hospital with complications from AIDS, his publicist announced, "His doctors have diagnosed that he has cancer of the liver and that it is not operable." When reporters asked directly about rumors Hudson had AIDS, the publicist told them, "The doctor…has seen no indication of AIDS." According to Hudson's official biographer, Sara Davidson, it was only after the hospital staff angrily threatened to reveal the truth themselves that the actor finally agreed to release a statement acknowledging his actual condition.

4. Amanda Blake (1925-1989), U.S. actress

The former star of *Gunsmoke* lied about her medical condition to all but her closest associates. According to one longtime friend who knew the truth, Blake didn't want to spend her final months in a media "goldfish bowl." Even after her death in August 1989, Blake's friends and doctors continued to mislead the public: Her death was officially attributed to cancer. It was only during a messy legal dispute over her estate several months later that the truth finally came out.

5. Roy Cohn (1927-1986), U.S. attorney

In 1985 the controversial New York attorney was asked on *60 Minutes* about rumors he was gay and dying of AIDS. "It's a lie as far as I'm concerned," Cohn replied. "I'll tell you categorically, I do not have AIDS." Cohn insisted he was suffering from liver cancer. He also lied to longtime friends and business associates. He told one friend, "If I had AIDS, I would have thrown myself out the window of the hospital.... I have liver cancer." After his death in July of 1986, it was revealed that Cohn had been suffering from "underlying HTLV-III infections."

6. Perry Ellis (1940-1986), U.S. fashion designer

Ellis was so ill at the preview of his fall and winter collection in 1986 that he could make only a brief appearance and had to be held up by two colleagues so that he could acknowledge the standing ovation he received. Throughout his illness Ellis steadfastly refused to concede he had AIDS. He claimed to be suffering from "viral encephalitis," which was also later announced as the cause of his death. One fashion industry spokesman explained, "Many people are making clothes for real macho types out there, and the last thing they want is to be associated with homosexuals and AIDS."

7. Michael Bennett (1943-1987), U.S. choreographer
After he was first diagnosed and became ill, Bennett lied and told friends and associates he was suffering from heart disease.

8. Freddie Mercury (1946-1991), British rock star
Mercury's health was the subject of speculation for months before his death. His gaunt and exhausted appearance at the 1990 British Phonographic Industry Awards only fueled the rumors. After a British newspaper published a photograph of him at the event, Mercury denied he had AIDS and said he'd never felt better in his life. The denials continued until November 23, 1991, when Mercury released a prepared press statement acknowledging the truth. "I felt it correct to keep this information private," he wrote, "in order to protect the privacy of those around me. However, the time has now come for my friends and fans around the world to know the truth, and I hope that everyone will join with me, my doctors, and all those worldwide in the fight against this terrible disease." The following day Mercury died of AIDS-related bronchial pneumonia.

9. Liberace (1919-1987), U.S. entertainer
Even as he lay dying of the disease at his home in Las Vegas, the entertainer denied reports he had AIDS. When, two weeks before his death, the *Las Vegas Sun* printed a story revealing the truth, his publicists continued to lie: They insisted that his recent weight loss and shocking pallor were the result of a misguided new diet that consisted almost exclusively of eating watermelon. Even his death certificate obfuscated the truth by making no mention of AIDS, a fact that, when made public, ignited a national controversy over the underreporting of AIDS-related deaths in the United States.

10. Rene Enriquez (1943-1990), U.S. actor
The actor—best known as Lt. Ray Calletano on the hit TV series *Hill Street Blues*—first learned he had AIDS in 1987. However, he decided to tell most of his family, friends, and coworkers that he was suffering from pancreatic cancer. When he died in 1990, his two sisters—who knew the truth—had his body swiftly cremated in hopes of continuing the deception. However, the real

cause of his death—AIDS-related cytomegalovirus enteritis—eventually came out in the press. Many of his friends and entertainment associates expressed shock and frustration that he had not trusted them with the truth.

11. Terry Dolan (1950-1986), U.S. political lobbyist
Dolan—a conservative activist and outspoken "family values" advocate who helped push the Reagan agenda of the 1980s—lied repeatedly, both privately and in public, about his homosexuality and his declining health from AIDS. He insisted he was suffering from complications of diabetes. Shortly after Dolan's death from AIDS complications in 1986, *The Washington Post* revealed the truth. His equally conservative brother, Reagan speechwriter Anthony Dolan, took umbrage at the public revelation and immediately bought a two-page newspaper ad to angrily denounce the *Post* and what he described as the "homosexual intrigue" of the liberal media.

9 Gay Teachers

1. Socrates (469-399 B.C.)
Greek philosopher and teacher whose noble life and courageous death have made him one of the most admired figures in history. Socrates exploited the Athenian homosexual ethos as a basis of metaphysical doctrine and philosophical method.

2. Plato (428-347 B.C.)
One of the most important thinkers and writers in the history of Western culture, Plato founded the Academy, an interdisciplinary school for research. Plato's teachings and writings take homosexual desire and homosexual love as the starting point from which to develop metaphysical theory.

3. Brunetto Latini (1220-1295)
Florentine tutor of Dante. In *The Divine Comedy,* Dante praised

his teacher for his "dear, kind and paternal countenance." Despite the accolades, however, Dante condemned Latini to the third round of the seventh circle of hell, a place reserved for sodomites.

4. Goldsworthy Dickinson (1862-1932)
English philosopher and lecturer at Kings College, Dickinson was a founder of the League of Nations. His 1896 masterpiece, *The Greek Way of Life,* as well as later writings on love between people of the same sex, gave indications that, as E.M. Forster later wrote, "all his deepest emotions were towards men."

5. Ludwig Wittgenstein (1889-1951)
Anglo-Austrian schoolmaster Wittgenstein's 1922 book *Tractatus Logico-Philosophicus* brought about a revolution in modern philosophy. Until recently biographers have bent over backward to avoid confronting his homosexuality and his long-term relationship with Francis Skinner.

6. F. O. Matthiessen (1902-1950)
Harvard professor whose courses on American literature and the criticism of poetry made him the Ivy League's model of tutorial talent and commitment. The candid love letters between Matthiessen and his partner of twenty years, Russell Cheney, were published in 1978.

7. Paul Goodman (1911-1972)
Lecturer, dissident, and author of *Growing Up Absurd,* Goodman claimed his homosexuality inspired his libertarian sense of humanity and a sense of beauty and democracy. But his unorthodox sexual behavior got him dismissed from a "progressive" boarding school.

8. Wing Biddlebaum (1919)
The small-town schoolteacher in Sherwood Anderson's *Winesburg, Ohio* was much loved by the boys of his school. A "half-wit" became enamored of him and in dreams imagined "unspeakable things" and went about telling them as fact. A mob ran Biddlebaum out of town. Anderson's story is the quintessential portrait of the homosexual teacher as victim.

9. **Eric Rofes (b. 1954)**
Rofes lost his sixth-grade teaching job in the suburbs of Boston after coming out as a gay activist. He was later hired by an innovative private school where, with his students, he produced the best-selling *The Kids' Book of Divorce.* He tells about his years as a closeted gay schoolteacher in *Socrates, Plato & Guys Like Me: Confessions of a Gay Schoolteacher.*

9 Contemporaries of Oscar Wilde and What Each Said About Him

1. **Walt Whitman, U.S. poet**
During his 1882 tour of America, Wilde met Whitman at Whitman's home in Camden, New Jersey. Whitman later said of him: "I took him up to my den where we had a jolly good time. I was glad to have him with me, for his youthful health, enthusiasm, and buoyancy are refreshing. He was in his best mood, and I imagine he laid aside any affectation he is said to have." Whitman found him "genuine, honest, and manly." Wilde, for his part, left behind a 10- by 12-inch framed photograph of himself inscribed simply, TO WALT FROM OSCAR.

2. **Jefferson Davis, U.S. soldier and statesman**
Davis's reaction to Wilde, after they met, at Wilde's insistence, in Mississippi in 1882, was characteristically terse. "I did not like the man," he said simply. Nonetheless, Wilde left Davis a framed, inscribed photograph of himself, just as he had with Whitman.

3. **George Bernard Shaw, British playwright**
Long an admirer of Wilde's plays, he tried, after Wilde's imprisonment, to circulate a petition calling for the suspension of Wilde's

sentence of two years' hard labor. Only two other people were willing to sign it. In *My Memories of Oscar Wilde,* Shaw wrote: "Please let us hear no more of the tragedy of Oscar Wilde. Oscar was no tragedian. He was the superb comedian of his century, one to whom misfortune, disgrace, imprisonment were external and traumatic. His gaiety of soul was invulnerable."

4. Henry James, U.S. author

While George Bernard Shaw's petition was unsuccessfully making the rounds in London, a similar petition was circulated by poet Stuart Merrill in the U.S. Among the people asked to sign it was novelist Henry James. He refused. James had met Wilde in Washington, D.C., in 1882. Far from being charmed by Wilde's wit and drollery, James was repulsed by Wilde's flippancy. He wrote a friend: "Oscar Wilde is here—an unclean beast." At various other times James referred to Wilde as "repulsive and fatuous," "a fatuous fool," and "a tenth-rate cad." He dismissed Wilde's plays as "cheap," "primitive," and "mechanical." Later, however, he did concede that Wilde's arrest and conviction were "hideously tragic" and that Wilde's imprisonment was "cruel." But still, he refused to sign a petition for Wilde's release.

5. John Addington Symonds, English author and historian

Although he was himself homosexual and although he and Wilde had once had a brief, amiable correspondence, Symonds did not care for Wilde's effete form of homosexuality. "I resent the unhealthy, scented, mystic, congested touch which a man of this sort has on moral problems," he wrote a friend.

6. Sir Arthur Conan Doyle, English author

The creator of Sherlock Holmes met Wilde in London at a dinner party arranged by a publisher. "It was a golden evening for me," Doyle later recalled. Wilde's conversation, he said, "left an indelible impression upon my mind. He towered above us all."

7. Willie Wilde, Oscar's brother
He once naively told George Bernard Shaw, "Oscar was not a man of bad character; you could trust him with a woman anywhere."

8. Viscount Castlerosse, English journalist
He became famous for his oft-quoted remark that Wilde was "every other inch a gentleman."

9. Colonel George Keppel, English aristocrat
He summed up the feelings of much of Britain's aristocracy when, shortly after Wilde's death, he dismissed Wilde as "a frightful bounder" and remarked, "It made me puke to look at him."

4 Gay Victims of the Nazis

1. Count Albrecht von Bernstorff (d. 1945)
The nephew of the German ambassador to the United States during World War I, von Bernstorff was a retired senior counselor at the German Foreign Ministry who used his personal and political connections to help Jews and other "undesirables" escape from the Nazi death machine. He was a member of the so-called Solf Circle, a group of aristocrats who opposed the oppression and savage persecution of human beings under the Nazi regime; they met regularly at the home of a Frau Anna Solf in Berlin. Von Bernstorff—monied, intelligent, middle-aged, and effetely homosexual—concentrated on getting Jews and other émigrés safely out of the country with their belongings. He also used his diplomatic connections to warn the Dutch government of Hitler's planned invasion of Holland in 1940. Because of these activities, he has since been called "one of the most courageous opponents of Hitler." In the autumn of 1943, von Bernstorff and the rest of the Solf Circle were betrayed by a Swiss doctor who came regularly to the anti-Nazi salons; the man, Dr. Reckse, was actually an informant for the Gestapo. Reckse offered to carry letters from the anti-Hitler con-

spirators to their friends and fellow resisters in Switzerland. Instead, he took the incriminating letters directly to Heinrich Himmler, and on January 12, 1944, all of the Circle's members were arrested. Von Bernstorff was incarcerated in Lehrterstrasse prison in Berlin. His life was spared for over a year because Himmler thought he might eventually prove useful. However, on April 23, 1945, with the Russians at the edge of the German capital, von Bernstorff was taken outside with several other prisoners and lined up against a wall. An SS detachment, acting on Himmler's orders, mowed them down with machine guns.

2. "Inga" (d. 1943)

Posthumously awarded the Order of St. Olav, the highest civilian honor that the King of Norway can confer on a Norwegian subject, Inga was a female impersonator who worked for the Resistance after the Nazis occupied Norway in 1940. His family had disowned him when they discovered he was gay, and he went to Oslo looking for work as a female impersonator in a local cabaret. After 1940 he became involved in the Resistance and used his convincing impersonations to slip back and forth across the border to Sweden with information on Nazi shipping movements in the North Sea; a woman aroused less suspicion than a man. In the autumn of 1943 he was returning from Sweden when he was attacked by a group of drunk Nazi soldiers at the border. After trying to rape him, they discovered he was a man. He was arrested, brutally tortured, and then executed. A portrait of him, in full drag, hangs today in the Resistance Museum in Oslo.

3. Maurice Sachs (d. 1944)

Eighteen-year-old Maurice Sachs served for a time as Jean Cocteau's secretary and errand boy. Sachs was dark-haired, disarming, and precociously talented with words. He wrote several novels and memoirs of life in Paris, many of which were published posthumously. Unfortunately, he was also self-destructive and untrustworthy with money. Living in Paris as a protégé of Cocteau, he misused the funds Coco Chanel gave him to assemble a library for her; he sold several valuable letters and documents from

Cocteau's apartment and pocketed the money for himself; and when he decided to join a seminary and become a priest (he was a convert from Judaism to Catholicism), his fellow seminarians soon had to fend off his numerous creditors who were banging at the seminary door demanding money. Sachs's vocation as a priest quickly crumbled when he fell in love with a teenage American boy vacationing on the Mediterranean; likewise, Sachs's marriage of convenience to an American woman crumbled several years later when he fell in love with a man in the United States and fled back to France with him.

Despite all of these embarrassments, there must have been something intensely likable about him: His friends, including Cocteau, forgave him time and again. As a homosexual of Jewish extraction, however, Sachs was in grave danger during the German occupation of France. At first he became romantically involved with a Nazi officer in Paris; the two of them lived together for a time. When the relationship soured, Sachs resorted to dealing in the black market in order to survive. Not long afterward he became entangled in a web of Gestapo intrigue and began working for the Nazis as an informer. He soon proved unreliable, however, and was finally condemned to a German prison. With the approach of the Allied forces, the prison was hastily evacuated, and the prisoners were sent on a grueling forced march across Germany. Anyone who stumbled or fell was shot in the back of the head. Sachs was one of those who did not make it.

4. Max Jacob (d. 1944)

One of the most richly creative French poets of the early twentieth century, Jacob numbered Cocteau, Picasso, and Natalie Barney among his numerous friends. Remembered as a gentle, charming, and considerate man, he was a regular contributor to Apollinaire's magazine *Les Soirees de Paris* and was a devoted mentor to numerous young protégés. It was he who "discovered" the sixteen-year-old enfant terrible Raymond Radiguet and introduced him to Cocteau. Born a Jew, Jacob converted to Christianity in 1909 and became a Catholic in 1915. In 1924 he retired from city life to the Benedictine abbey of St. Benoit-sur-Loire, where he lived, on and off, in seclusion for the next twenty years; he said he could not live in Paris without succumbing regularly to sexual temptation. He fervently desired to be a devout Catholic, partly because he had a terrible fear of suffering in hell. The cruel irony is that hell on earth was already at his doorstep, and in February 1944, when he was sixty-eight years old, he was abruptly arrested by the Gestapo. His brother, sister, and brother-in-law—all Jewish—had already perished in the death camps.

Jacob's commitment to Catholicism could not save him: He was a homosexual and of Jewish extraction. Shortly after his arrest, he managed to get a short note to Cocteau telling of his fate. "I embrace you," were his final words. Cocteau and others signed a petition to obtain his release, but without result. Jacob contracted pneumonia shortly after his internment in the concentration camp at Drancy, just outside of Paris. The Nazis refused him adequate medical treatment, and he perished.

7 Men Who Were Full- or Part-Time Transvestites

1. Jenny Savalette de Lange

Wandering about Paris and Versailles in her dated clothes and her wide-brimmed hats, the woman known as Jenny Savalette de Lange aroused little curiosity. She was, according to her contemporaries, no beauty: She was gaunt and tall, with hard features and a sullen look. She always carried an umbrella. When she died at Versailles on May 6, 1858, her body was quietly handed over to two old women to prepare it for burial. It was then discovered that Jenny was, in fact, a man.

Apparently, for almost seventy years, no one had known her secret; she had few friends, and she never married, though she reportedly had several lovers. She lived most of her life on a generous government pension, although no one could figure out exactly how she had gotten the pension in the first place or why.

Gossip soon began to spread that Jenny was actually Louis XVII, the son of Marie Antoinette and King Louis XVI. Captured by French revolutionaries along with his mother and father as they tried to flee France in 1791, the ten-year-old Louis had allegedly died in prison of tuberculosis shortly after his parents were guillotined. However, his last months in prison were veiled in secrecy, and for years afterward there were stories that the boy had actually escaped with the help of monarchists who planned to restore him one day as rightful heir to the throne of France. Over the years more than thirty people had claimed to be the young prince. In the case of Jenny Savalette de Lange, nothing could be proved, and the mystery was never solved, despite the efforts of numerous people to find out exactly who she was and where she had come from. Jenny's death certificate stated simply that she was "an unknown man…a bachelor."

2. Lord Cornbury

Cornbury served as colonial governor of New York and New Jersey between 1702 and 1709 and then as governor of North Carolina from 1711 to 1712. During his administrations he became notorious as both a drunkard and a transvestite: He was called "the governor in petticoats." Dressed one night in his wife's clothes, he was detained as a drunk vagrant by his own officers, who did not recognize him at first. On other occasions Cornbury allegedly paraded around the fort dressed in elaborate and sumptuous female attire, a distraction to all public business. He claimed that his transvestism was meant as a tribute to his cousin, Queen Anne. There is a portrait of him (currently owned by the New York Historical Society) in full drag—in a classic, unpretentious blue gown, long white gloves, and a small lace or ribbon topknot. His face was distinctly unattractive, with thick lips, carefully arched eyebrows, and double chin. Cornbury was one of the most corrupt and despised public officials of his day; his political career apparently ended in 1712, and he died in 1723 at the age of sixty-two.

3. Barbette

"Unforgettable." "A theatrical masterpiece." "An angel, a flower, a bird." That was how Jean Cocteau described Barbette, the female impersonator whose act at the Casino de Paris became the toast of Paris in the late 1920s. An accomplished acrobat and tightrope dancer, Barbette would first appear onstage in a sumptuous evening gown, usually of lamés and paillettes, with trimmings of feathers and lace. The evening gown was soon removed, revealing beneath it the outfit of a woman trapeze artist. Accompanied by the music of Wagner and Rimsky-Korsakov, Barbette would then mount the high-wire or trapeze and swing and dance in midair high above the audience's heads. The ten-minute act always ended the same way, with a touch of high drama—descending from the trapeze and moving toward the audience, Barbette would dramatically remove his wig and reveal that he was a man. The routine became legendary in various European capitals—among them Berlin, Warsaw, Madrid, and Copenhagen—and he was admired not only by Cocteau but also by Igor Stravinsky and numerous other composers, artists, and writers of the day.

Barbette's background seemed slightly incongruous for the glamour of the Casino de Paris. Born Vander Clyde in a small town in Texas in 1904, he got his start as a trapeze artist in San Antonio, before he began to develop his own solo act disguised as a woman. After performing across the United States, he signed with the William Morris Agency and was sent to England and Paris in the fall of 1923, where his performances were received as a theatrical tour de force. "I myself have seen no comparable display of artistry on the stage since Nijinsky," Cocteau wrote a friend. After more than a decade of popular acclaim, Barbette's spectacular career ended abruptly when he became ill with a sudden crippling affliction of the bones and joints. He returned to Texas, where he worked as an acrobatic trainer. Barbette can be seen, briefly, as a lady in a theater box in Jean Cocteau's 1930 film *Blood of a Poet.* His theatrical career provided part of the inspiration for Blake Edwards's 1982 musical-comedy *Victor/Victoria.*

4. Stella Walsh

An Olympic gold medalist in track and field, Stella Walsh was considered one of the most formidable woman runners of the 1930s. During the 1932 and 1936 Olympics, she won a total of five gold medals, along with three silver and one bronze. Later she married and retired to a suburb of Cleveland, where she dedicated herself to working with children in athletics. To the people who knew her, it came as a shock when, in 1981, she was robbed and shot to death in a department store parking lot. It came as an even greater shock to the sports world when, during preparations for the funeral, it was discovered that Stella Walsh was a man.

Born Stanislawa Walaslewicz in Poland in 1911, Walsh had often aroused comment during competition in the 1930s for her extraordinary musculature and excessive body hair; it was often remarked that she ran like a man. In 1956, having retired from competition, Walsh married Harry Olson in Las Vegas; they separated after eight weeks but never divorced. After Walsh's death Olson said he was surprised by the report of his wife's true sex. He told the press that he and Walsh had had sex only "a couple of times, and she wouldn't let me have any lights on." Despite the revelation that Walsh was a man, the U.S. Olympic Committee announced there would be no attempt to posthumously retract Walsh's Olympic medals.

5. Alexander Woollcott

The acerbic theater critic and unctuous radio sage of the 1920s, '30s, and early '40s was a pampered child whose sisters incessantly dressed him as a girl. He founded his college's first dramatic club but demanded that he play all of the feminine leads in its productions. After that he started appearing at parties dressed in women's clothes and often handed out calling cards that read, ALEXANDRA WOOLLCOTT. Secretly he was tormented by his confused sexual feelings. His torment was aggravated by the taunts of his classmates. "I wonder if he has to sit down to pee," said one. Others called him "freak" or "sissy." By his sophomore year Woollcott seriously considered suicide.

The torment and confusion lasted well into his adult life. After he achieved fame as a journalist and a theater critic, he invited playwright Anita Loos to his home one afternoon and showed her a picture of himself dressed as a woman in college. He confessed, with tears in his eyes, that he had always wanted to be a girl. "All my life I've wanted to be a mother," he added sorrowfully. Described by Edna Ferber as "that New Jersey Nero who thinks his pinafore is a toga," Woollcott later made a profitable hobby of designing women's clothing. At home he often appeared to guests dressed in vast flowing dressing gowns and huge wide-brimmed hats. By then he was hideously overweight, and in these bizarre getups he often looked, according to friend Harpo Marx, "like something that had gotten loose from Macy's Thanksgiving Day parade."

6. Magnus Hirschfeld

Once described as "the Einstein of sex," Hirschfeld was a short, pudgy, effeminate neurologist who, in late-nineteenth-century Germany, became a leading pioneer in the fledgling field of sexual research. Independently wealthy, he was free to devote himself to writing, education, and working for legal reforms. In 1897 he founded one of the first organizations to defend homosexuals' rights, the Scientific Humanitarian Committee, which was devoted to repealing harsh antigay laws in the German penal code. In 1919 he founded the world's first sex research institute, the Institute of Sexual Science in Berlin, which was a repository for books, magazines, pictures, personal testimonies, and other scientific material dealing with sex.

Because of his research and because he was Jewish, Hirschfeld was reviled by the Nazis; in 1933 they ransacked his institute and burned much of its priceless collection of over 20,000 volumes and 35,000 pictures. Hirschfeld himself was once severely beaten and left for dead by a group of Nazis on a street in Munich. He was forced to flee the country and died in France in 1935.

Hirschfeld was both gay and a transvestite. In fact, he coined the word *transvestism.* "Beneath the duality of sex there is a oneness," he once wrote. "Every male is potentially a female and every female potentially a male. If a man wants to understand a woman, he must discover the woman in himself, and if a woman would understand a man, she must dig in her own consciousness to discover her own masculine traits."

7. Ed Wood Jr.

Wood was credited with making more awful movies than any other film director in Hollywood, and his 1959 opus, *Plan 9 From Outer Space* (starring Bela Lugosi, former professional wrestler Tor Johnson, gay psychic Criswell, and '50s pop icon Vampira) has consistently been voted, by critics and cinephiles alike, the worst motion picture of all time.

Wood never intended to make bad films. In fact, he actually believed in what he was doing. His 1953 directorial debut, *Glen or Glenda*—the saga of a heterosexual man tormented by a desire to wear his girlfriend's clothing—was, in his mind, a heartfelt plea for tolerance for transvestites. It was a subject close to Wood's heart. Wood, himself a transvestite, had scripted the film and then cast himself in the title role (under the stage name Daniel Davis). He even persuaded his real-life girlfriend, part-time actress Dolores Fuller, to appear opposite him. (Dolores found out about Wood's transvestism only when she read the script for the film for the first time. Despite her initial outrage and perplexity, she still agreed to make the picture.) Wood directed much of *Glen or Glenda* while dressed in women's clothing, a habit he maintained throughout his career; whenever work on one of his film projects wasn't going well, he retreated to a dressing room and donned female clothes to relax and think more clearly. Or, as the narrator of *Glen or Glenda* explained: "Give this man satin undies, a dress, a sweater, and a skirt, or even the lounging outfit he has on, and he's the happiest man in the world. He can work better, he can think better, he can play better. And he can be more of a credit to his community and his government."

After directing his last motion picture, *The Sinister Urge,* in 1961, Wood languished in obscurity for years. He wrote scripts for two other films—*Orgy of the Dead* and *Fugitive Girls*—but movie work of any kind was increasingly difficult to find. He drank himself to death, at the age of 54, in 1978. The man who would later be voted "The Worst Director of All Time" barely rated an obituary in *Variety.*

14 Men Who Loved Boys

1. Episthenes (4th century B.C.), Greek soldier
He tried to intervene in the public execution of a remarkably handsome teenage boy he had never seen before. Totally captivated by the youth's looks and anguished at the thought of such beauty being destroyed, Episthenes begged the executioner to stop and offered his own life in place of the boy's. After some discussion, in which friends testified to Episthenes' bravery in battle and his passion for beautiful boys, the handsome youth was spared, and Episthenes walked off with him.

2. Demetrius I (336-283 B.C.), Macedonian king
He was so enamored of a beautiful Greek youth named Damocles that he followed the teenager everywhere, hoping to seduce him. The boy, however, was known not only for his beauty but also for his virtue, and he fled in horror from the king's relentless sexual advances. Finally, tracked down and cornered in a public bathhouse by the king, Damocles quickly searched for a means of escape. Finding none, he jumped into a cauldron of boiling water rather than compromise himself—a suicide that Plutarch later called "untimely and unmerited, but worthy of the beauty that occasioned it."

3. Catullus (84-54 B.C.), Roman poet
In his poems he liked to boast of his conquests of teenage boys and bragged that he once, after surprising a boy and girl in the act of making love, mounted the boy "to please Venus." Disappointed in love by the beautiful nymphomaniac Clodia, he turned to an equally beautiful boy, Juventius. However, Juventius was fickle and cruel, and the affair was stormy, to say the least. Catullus, who was barely thirty when he died, expressed disgust for most homosexuals, except those who were active lovers of boys.

4. Nero (A.D. 37-68), Roman emperor
He tried to turn one of his slave boys, Sporus, into a girl by castration, then went through a public wedding ceremony with him—dowry, bridal veil, and all. A popular joke at the time was that the world would have been a happier place had Nero's father, Domitius, married that sort of wife.

5. Strato (2nd century), Greek poet
One of the most cheerfully gluttonous boy chasers of the ancient world, Strato was the editor and primary author of the *Musa Puerilis,* an anthology of over two hundred epigrams devoted to the subject of boy-love. He blithely confessed, in one poem, that "I like a boy's body when he's hot from the park, and his flesh glistens with oil. I like a boy with grime on his body, not with the pretty enchantment of the romantics."

6. Leonardo da Vinci (1452-1519), Italian artist and inventor
At the age of 38, Leonardo "adopted" a beautiful but roguish ten-year-old boy, nicknamed Salai, "Little Devil." His presence in Leonardo's home has perplexed scholars for centuries, since Salai was neither exactly a servant nor an apprentice and since Leonardo himself described the boy (always with a certain exasperated affection) as a "thieving, lying, obstinate" glutton. In his journals Leonardo kept an exact running tally of everything the boy stole: money from friends, money from Leonardo's wallet, boots, silver. The boy grew into a handsome and charming young man, but he was still a thief and a liar. He had a taste for beautiful clothes, especially shoes. According to one of Leonardo's biographers, Salai owned "quite a fantastic number of pairs of shoes." Leonardo and the boy remained inseparable companions for nearly twenty-six years.

7. Michelangelo (1475-1564), Italian sculptor and painter
Michelangelo was in his late sixties when he met Cecchino dei Bracci, the charming and beautiful fifteen-year-old nephew of one of his friends. Of the boy's beauty, he wrote: "With his face God wished to correct nature." When Bracci died in 1544, at the age of sixteen, Michelangelo designed the boy's tomb and wrote no

fewer than fifty poems mourning his passing. Other boys thought to have been Michelangelo's lovers were: Gherardo Perini, a muscular, strikingly beautiful young male model whose relationship with Michelangelo was the subject of much gossip at the time; Tommaso Cavalieri, an intelligent and handsome young nobleman who remained one of Michelangelo's lifelong friends; and Febo di Poggio, a young male prostitute of whom Michelangelo wrote, "Up from the earth I rose with his wings, and death itself I could have found sweet."

8. Christopher Marlowe (1564-1593), English dramatist
Marlowe's tastes were best characterized by his famous epigram, "All they that love not tobacco and boys are fools."

9. Horatio Alger (1834-1899), U.S. novelist
As pastor of the Unitarian Church in Brewster, Massachusetts, he befriended many of the local boys and took them on seaside picnics. Two of the boys eventually stepped forward and confessed that they had engaged in homosexual acts with the 34-year-old Alger. Confronted, Alger did not deny it. He was run out of town and fled to New York City, where he achieved national fame writing stories for boys. He later became a tireless philanthropist working to improve conditions for homeless youths, orphans, and runaways.

10. Oscar Wilde (1854-1900), Irish dramatist and wit
Wilde claimed to prefer lower-class boys because "their passion was all body and no soul." He once bragged to a friend of having made love to five different boys in a single night. "I kissed each one of them in every part of their bodies," he said. "They were all dirty and appealed to me just for that reason."

11. Friedrich Alfred Krupp (1854-1902), German industrialist
The multimillionaire German industrialist set up a lavish private pleasure palace in a grotto on the Italian island of Capri, where he entertained underage Italian boys, mostly the sons of local fishermen. Sex was performed to the accompaniment of a live string quartet, and orgasms were celebrated with bursts of fireworks.

When Krupp's wife, back home in Germany, heard rumors of what was going on, she went straight to the Kaiser—who promptly had her committed to an insane asylum. The Krupp industrialist empire was too vital to German national security to be compromised by such stories, even if true. However, the German press eventually found out about Krupp's private orgies and printed the whole story, complete with damning photographs taken by Krupp himself inside the grotto. Rather than face disgrace, Krupp committed suicide.

12. Constantine Cavafy (1863-1933), Greek poet
Living in Alexandria, Egypt, he frequented houses of prostitution where strong, well-built Greek boys (most of them poor and with wretched jobs during the day) earned extra money having sex with older men. He bribed his servants to ruffle up his bedsheets so that his mother wouldn't suspect he had been out all night.

13. André Gide (1869-1951), French writer
Having lost his virginity at the age of twenty-three to a fourteen-year-old Arab youth in Tunisia, he later fell in love with a fifteen-year-old servant boy in Algeria. Gide longed to take the boy back with him to France, but Gide's mother opposed the idea: She couldn't stand the idea of a "Negro," as she called him, living with them in Paris. When he was forty-seven, Gide fell in love and had an affair with sixteen-year-old Marc Allegret.

14. William S. Burroughs (b. 1914), U.S. writer
Laid up in a hospital in Tangier, he used to fantasize about the boys at an Italian school across the street and often watched them with his binoculars. On another occasion he and a friend paid two Arab boys sixty cents to have sex in front of them. "We demanded semen too," Burroughs later wrote, "no half-assed screwing." Burroughs has said that "homosexuality is a worldwide economic fact. In poor countries—like Morocco and parts of Italy—it's one of the big industries, one of the main ways in which a young boy can get somewhere."

15 Gay or Bisexual Fathers

1. Alexander the Great (356-323 B.C.), Macedonian ruler
Alexander had one son, the result of his marriage to an Asian princess. In the power struggle and bloodbath that followed Alexander's death, the boy, who was only thirteen, was murdered.

2. Edward II (1284-1327), king of England
Despite his almost exclusively homosexual nature, Edward dutifully produced a male heir by his queen, Isabella. In 1327 Edward was deposed and brutally murdered by Isabella and her lover, Roger Mortimer. Edward's son, then only fifteen, became king of England—a puppet king until, just three years later, he asserted his independence, had Mortimer executed, and sent his scheming mother into retirement.

3. Il Sodoma (1477-1549), Italian painter
His name says it all: The High Renaissance painter gained a wide reputation during his lifetime as a homosexual. But Il Sodoma still found the energy to father a daughter, Faustina. Faustina married one of her father's former boyfriends.

4. James I (1566-1625), king of England
Knowledge of James's homosexuality was so widespread that when he succeeded Elizabeth I as monarch of England, people shouted in the streets, "Elizabeth was King, now James is Queen!" In his lifetime James produced a daughter and two male heirs. His younger son ascended to the throne as Charles I in 1625. James was himself the son of a homosexual father, the notorious profligate Lord Darnley, second husband of Mary, Queen of Scots.

5. Walt Whitman (1819-1892), U.S. poet
Whitman claimed to have fathered at least six illegitimate children and wove rather fantastic and sometimes inconsistent stories about them. Some historians dismiss the claim as defensive bravado,

Whitman's anxious answer to those who tried to label him homosexual. Others are not quite so sure, although no trace of the children has ever been discovered.

6. John Addington Symonds (1840-1893), English essayist and historian

In spite of his lifelong obsession with homosexuality and his dalliances with gondoliers, college boys, and the like, Symonds remained married for twenty-eight years. "Our domestic relations are not of the happiest," he discreetly wrote a friend, "and we get along best when we are away from one another." Symonds had four daughters. When Symonds's unpublished, explicitly homoerotic memoirs were sealed in the London Library after his death, his youngest daughter, Katharine, was the first person to ask permission to read them.

7. Paul Verlaine (1844-1896), French poet

Verlaine had one son, Georges, whom he abused as an infant and neglected as a young adult. An alcoholic, Georges led a pathetic, listless life, before dying of drink in 1926 at the age of fifty-four.

8. Oscar Wilde (1854-1900), Irish playwright and wit

Wilde married when he was twenty-nine and had two sons, Cyril and Vyvyan. After Wilde was sentenced in 1895 to two years' hard labor for having committed homosexual acts, his wife took the boys, then aged eight and nine, to Switzerland and changed the family name. "That the law should decide and take upon itself that I am unfit to be with my own children is something quite horrible to me," Wilde wrote in *De Profundis.* "The disgrace of prison is as nothing compared to it." After his release Wilde petitioned his wife, unsuccessfully, for permission to see the boys, but she would only send him photographs of them. "I want my boys," he wrote in anguish to a friend. As it turned out, Wilde saw neither his wife nor his sons ever again. He died in exile in Paris in 1900. The younger son, Vyvyan, later wrote several favorable books about his father, including *Son of Oscar Wilde* and *A Pictorial Biography of Oscar Wilde.*

9. **André Gide (1869-1951), French author**
Gide was fifty-four when he fathered an illegitimate daughter, Catherine; the mother was Elisabeth van Bysselberghe, a well-known feminist. Gide lived to be eighty-two, long enough to see himself a grandfather.

10. **Lord Alfred Douglas (1870-1945), English poet**
After his fateful friendship with Oscar Wilde ended in scandal, Douglas renounced homosexuality and became a fervent convert to the Roman Catholic church. Two years after Wilde's death, Douglas married Olive Custance, a minor poetess, and they had one son, Raymond. Olive's father, Colonel Custance, took a dim view of Douglas as both a husband and a parent. Alleging that Douglas was a cruel and irresponsible father—certainly on the basis of Douglas's notorious relationship with Wilde—the Colonel successfully sued to have young Raymond taken away from his parents. The Colonel's action tore Douglas's marriage apart, as poor Olive sided first with her father, then with her husband, then with her father again. The marriage ended in a shambles, and Douglas's attempts to win back custody of his son were unsuccessful. The custody battles and family rifts took their toll on little Raymond: He grew up with severe emotional problems. At the age of twenty-five he was diagnosed as schizophrenic and was committed to a private mental hospital. He spent much of his life in and out of such institutions and died in one in 1964.

11. **W. Somerset Maugham (1874-1965), English author**
Maugham once said of himself, "I tried to persuade myself that I was three-quarters normal and that only a quarter of me was queer—whereas really it was the other way around." In 1915 Maugham fathered an illegitimate daughter, Elizabeth; two years later he married the girl's mother. The marriage was a tragic, bitter mistake. Maugham angrily told his wife: "I married you because I thought it the best thing for your happiness and for Elizabeth's welfare, but I did not marry you because I loved you, and you were only too aware of that." They were divorced in 1929, and young Elizabeth grew up to despise her famous father. When

Maugham was eighty-eight, Elizabeth tried to have him put away on the grounds that he was senile and incompetent. Maugham retaliated by legally disowning her and adopting his lover, Alan Searle, as his son. In court Elizabeth had the adoption nullified and was restored as Maugham's legal heir.

12. Vaslav Nijinsky (1890-1950), Russian dancer
Isadora Duncan once suggested to Nijinsky that he father her next child; he said no. For one thing, he was already involved in a sexual relationship, an intense and possessive one, with dance impresario Serge Diaghilev. However, in 1913 Nijinsky abruptly turned his back on Diaghilev—on homosexuality in general—and impulsively married the daughter of a Hungarian actress during a dance tour in South America. They had two daughters, remaining married until Nijinsky's death thirty-seven years later. In 1980, when Herbert Ross's film biography *Nijinsky* opened, one of Nijinsky's daughters, Kyra, then in her sixties, condemned it. She was particularly annoyed at the film's emphasis on her father's love affair with Diaghilev. "I certainly am not the child of my father and Diaghilev!" she indignantly reminded the press.

13. Leonard Bernstein (1918-1990), U.S. conductor and composer
Although he was, in the words of one of his biographers, Joan Peyser, "rampantly homosexual" for the early part of his life, Bernstein married in 1951 when he was in his early thirties. He and wife Felicia had three children: two girls and a boy. According to Peyser, Bernstein was again "promiscuously homosexual" during the later years of his life.

14. Yukio Mishima (1925-1970), Japanese author
Mishima had two children, both of whom are still living.

15. Jann Wenner (b. 1946), U.S. magazine publisher
The father of three children and the founder and publisher of *Rolling Stone* magazine, Wenner ignited a storm of gossip and speculation when he left his longtime wife and business partner, Jane, in 1994 for another man, Calvin Klein fashion executive Matt Nye.

10 Well-Known Women Who Married Gay or Bisexual Men

1. Angela Lansbury (b. 1925), U.S. actress
Her first marriage, in 1945, when she was nineteen, was to Richard Cromwell, a 35-year-old Hollywood actor who had appeared in over two dozen films, including *The Lives of a Bengal Lancer* and *Jezebel.* The marriage lasted barely eight months. It ended after she found him with another man and he acknowledged he was homosexual. Though soon divorced, they remained friends until his death in 1960 from cancer.

2. Carson McCullers (1917-1967), U.S. writer
She married Reeves McCullers in 1937, when she was nineteen, divorced him five years later, then remarried him in 1945. The marriage disintegrated the first time when they both fell in love with the same man, composer David Diamond. After their remarriage, Reeves became increasingly tormented, not only by his homosexual feelings but also by feelings of living in his wife's shadow. He began contemplating suicide and decided to take her with him. When he was driving her to a doctor's appointment one day, she noticed two lengths of coiled rope on the floorboard. "We're going out into the forest," he told her, "and hang ourselves. But first we'll stop and buy a bottle of brandy. We'll drink it for old times' sake." When he stopped at a liquor store, she fled the car. She never saw him again. Two months later he committed suicide with an overdose of barbiturates.

3. Vanessa Redgrave (b. 1937), British actress
Redgrave was married for a time during the 1960s to bisexual British film director Tony Richardson (*Tom Jones, The Loved One*). Richardson, with whom she had two children—Natasha and Joely, both actresses also—died of AIDS complications in 1991. Vanessa's father, the distinguished actor Sir Michael Redgrave, was also bisexual.

4. Annabella (b. 1909), French actress
She married actor Tyrone Power in 1939. They were divorced in 1948.

5. Mary, Queen of Scots (1542-1587)
Her second husband was the strikingly handsome Lord Darnley, a cousin. She was twenty-three; he was only twenty. Although she married him for love, it was a tragic choice: Darnley, though muscular and exceptionally good-looking, was emotionally weak and vicious, and although he provided her with an heir—the future James I of England—he apparently preferred sodomizing his young grooms and stableboys. Mary's love soon withered into contempt, and barely two years after they were married, Darnley was strangled to death, most likely by a conspiracy of nobles; he was allegedly having sex with one of his pages at the time.

6. Lillian Russell (1861-1922), U.S. singer and actress
She was married four times. Her third marriage was to gay tenor Giovanni Perugini. Friends described the union as "a marriage of convenience—his." It didn't last long. She resented his nagging, his violent outbursts, and his insults. The marriage ended after less than two months, after he tried to throw her from a seventh-story window. Defending the action, Perugini told a reporter, "Do you realize the enormity of this woman's offense—her crime? Do you know what she did to me? Why, sir, she took all the pillows; she used my rouge; she misplaced my manicure set; she used my special handkerchief perfume for her bath.... Once she threatened to spank me, and she did, with a hairbrush too. You can't expect a fellow to take a spanking with equanimity, can you?"

7. Vera Panova (1905-1973), Soviet writer
As an officially esteemed novelist and playwright in the Soviet Union, she extended whatever protection she could to her many gay friends and associates, including her own husband, writer David Dar, who publicly revealed his homosexuality after he had emigrated to Israel in 1977.

8. Ruth Warrick (b. 1915), U.S. actress
Warrick—best known for her portrayal of the first Mrs. Charles Foster Kane—married handsome character actor and radio announcer Erik Rolf in 1938, when she was twenty-two. It was a tumultuous and often unhappy marriage from the start, and during the course of it, Warrick consoled herself with affairs with Anthony Quinn, Douglas Fairbanks Jr., and others. In 1945 she and Rolf separated. It was only then that he confessed he had also been having extramarital affairs—with men. "I was deeply wounded," she said later, "but I had two beautiful children, and so I couldn't repudiate him." They divorced soon afterward.

9. Ruth St. Denis (1878-1968), U.S. dancer
Her husband was dancer Ted Shawn, renowned as "the father of American dance," with whom she founded Denishawn, the innovative American school and dance company that produced such illustrious pupils as Martha Graham. Although they remained married for over fifty years, they separated after seventeen, when they both fell in love with the same young man. Shawn blamed the sudden, overwhelming onset of his homosexuality on her numerous infidelities.

10. Elsa Lanchester (1902-1986), English actress
Her husband, actor Charles Laughton, revealed his homosexuality to her two years after they were married. She went deaf for a week after he made the announcement. However, she soon recovered, and they remained married for thirty-three years—no longer lovers, but still close friends and companions—until Laughton's death from bone cancer in 1962. They starred together in more than half a dozen films, including *Rembrandt, The Private Life of Henry VIII,* and *Witness for the Prosecution.*

10 Gay Men Who Didn't Let Advancing Age Stop Them

1. Alexander von Humboldt (1769-1859), German explorer and scientist

At the age of sixty he was exploring uncharted remote areas of Russia, Siberia, and Central Asia. The last twenty-five years of his life, beginning when he was sixty-five, were devoted to writing *Kosmos,* a four-volume scientific compendium for the general public. He was actively at work on a fifth volume to the series when he died suddenly at the age of ninety.

2. George Cukor (1899-1983), U.S. film director

Cukor was seventy-three when he directed the motion picture *Travels With My Aunt,* seventy-six when he directed *The Blue Bird,* and seventy-nine when he directed the critically acclaimed made-for-TV movie *The Corn Is Green,* with Katharine Hepburn. He directed his last film, *Rich and Famous,* when he was eighty-one.

3. Michelangelo (1475-1564), Italian sculptor and painter

He completed the tomb of Julius II when he was seventy. Six days before his death, at the age of eighty-eight, he was still at work sculpting the *Rondanini Pieta.*

4. Edward Everett Horton (1886-1970), U.S. actor

A veteran of over eighty films beginning in the early 1920s, Horton continued to work throughout his seventies and into his eighties. His last film, *Cold Turkey,* was made in 1970, when he was eighty-four.

5. Camille Saint-Saens (1835-1921), French composer

When he was eighty he was sent by the French government to the Panama-Pacific Exposition, where he was guest conductor of a series of concerts. At eighty-six he was still touring to perform his works.

6. George Santayana (1863-1952), Spanish philosopher
When Santayana was in his early eighties, he was immersed in the writing of *Dominations and Powers,* an analysis of man in society. At the age of eighty-eight he began work on a translation of Lorenzo de Medici's love poem "Ambra."

7. E.M. Forster (1879-1970), English writer
Forster was in his seventies when he wrote, with Eric Crozier, the libretto for Benjamin Britten's opera *Billy Budd.* At the age of eighty he was still reviewing books for the *Spectator* and the *Observer.* At eighty-one he appeared as a witness in the impassioned obscenity trial of D.H. Lawrence's *Lady Chatterley's Lover.*

8. Edward Carpenter (1844-1929), English writer and reformer
At seventy-one, Carpenter wrote *The Healing of Nations,* a denunciation of war. At seventy-three he wrote *Three Ballads,* a collection of satirical pieces. At seventy-four he edited *Poems Written During the Great War 1914-1918* and translated many of the poems included.

9. André Gide (1869-1951), French writer
He was in his mid seventies when he wrote *Theseus,* his last great literary work. At the age of seventy-eight, Gide won the Nobel Prize for literature. At the age of eighty-one, he published the final volume of his *Journal.*

10. Harry Hay (b. 1912), U.S. gay rights activist
When he was sixty-six, Hay cofounded the gay spiritual movement known as the Radical Faeries. Throughout his seventies he traveled widely and gave lectures across the country on gay activism as well as on gay spirituality. At seventy-four he was the grand marshall of the Long Beach gay pride parade. His lifelong motto has been, Above all, audacity.

8 Instances of Gay Lovers Buried Together

1. Robert de Montesquioi and Gabriel d'Yturri
For twenty years Gabriel d'Yturri was secretary and lover to French poet Robert de Montesquioi, the model for Baron de Charlus in Proust's *Remembrance of Things Past.* D'Yturri died in 1905 of complications from diabetes. His last words to de Montesquioi, before lapsing into a coma, were, "Thank you for teaching me to understand all these beautiful things." Sixteen years later, de Montesquioi died of kidney disease. In accordance with his instructions, he was buried beside d'Yturri in a cemetery at Versailles.

2. Robert Ross and Oscar Wilde
Wilde died in Paris in 1900, and his remains were temporarily buried in a small cemetery at Bagneux, before being moved nine years later to a permanent tomb at Pere Lachaise Cemetery in Paris. In 1950, during a ceremony commemorating the fiftieth anniversary of Wilde's death, the tomb was opened, and the ashes of Wilde's longtime friend and literary executor, Robert Ross, were placed inside. Ross had died in 1918; he had often claimed that he was "the first boy Oscar ever had."

3. Croce-Spinelli and Sivel
Croce-Spinelli and Sivel were two nineteenth-century balloonists who died together in a ballooning accident 26,000 feet over India in 1875; they were asphyxiated when the air grew too thin. The huge marble monument over the tomb they share in Pere Lachaise Cemetery portrays the men lying together side by side, hand in hand, presumably naked but covered by a sculpted sheet from the waist down. There are flowers in their hands. The tomb, one of the most talked-about monuments in Pere Lachaise, has been called a "tribute to their comradeship in life and death."

4. Conradin of Sicily and Frederick of Baden

Sixteen-year-old Conradin of Sicily was the last of the Hohenstaufen kings. Betrayed in his attempts to hold on to his crown, the adolescent king was beheaded by political enemies in 1268. His 21-year-old lover and adviser, Frederick of Baden, voluntarily joined him on the scaffold. The two lovers were interred together in the church of the monastery of Santa Maria del Carmine in Naples. For centuries after, the burial place was a shrine for gay lovers, and in 1847 the Crown Prince of Bavaria commissioned a marble statue to be erected there in Conradin's memory.

5. Epaminondas and two young soldiers

After being killed in the battle of Mantinea, the Theban general Epaminondas (418-362 B.C.) was buried in a tomb with two young soldiers who had been his lovers and who had also fallen in battle.

6. Benjamin Britten and Peter Pears

British composer Benjamin Britten died in 1976. Tenor Peter Pears, Britten's lover and collaborator for over forty years, died ten years later of a heart attack. Pears was laid to rest next to Britten in a grave in Aldeburgh, England.

7. Paul Monette and Roger Horwitz

Monette brilliantly chronicled the struggle and death from AIDS complications of his longtime lover Roger Horwitz in the book *Borrowed Time.* Horwitz died in 1986 and was buried in Forest Lawn Memorial Park in Los Angeles's Hollywood Hills, with the epitaph, WE SAIL TOGETHER, IF WE SAIL AT ALL. Monette died nine years later and was buried next to Horwitz.

8. William M. Evans and Dr. John T. Wells

The official history of the Lone Fir Cemetery, the oldest cemetery in Portland, Oregon, includes the listing: "In 1880 William M. Evans, a young lawyer, was taken sick with typhoid and pneumonia. He was attended by his dearest friend, Dr. John T. Wells, of the United States Navy. When Evans breathed his last, the physician wept at his bedside. The two men…had come to the Northwest together. Soon after his friend's death, Dr. Wells also passed away. The bodies of the two men lie side by side in Lone Fir Cemetery."

Index

Adventures of Priscilla, Queen of the Desert, The, 137-139
Agathocles, 85
AIDS, 21, 25, 27, 28, 38, 117, 118, 121-122, 151, 159, 162; people who lied about having, 167-171; porn stars who died from, 167
Air Force, gays who served in, 32
Albee, Edward, 80
Alexander the Great, 19, 188
Alger, Horatio, 154, 186
Alley, Kirstie, 24
Almodóvar, Pedro, 7
Anaphrodisiacs, 78
Andrews, Julie, 22-23
Angelou, Maya, 116
Animals, 3-5, 70-72, 88-89
Annabella, 193
Aphrodisiacs, people who believed in, 78-80; substances reputed to be, 75-78
Arbuckle, Fatty, 87
Aristotle, 78
Armey, Richard, 62
Army, gays or bisexuals who served in, 32
Arrests, on gay sex charges, 45, 46, 104, 110-115
Arthur, Chester, 42
Asner, Edward, 116
Astin, Patty Duke, 116
Astor, Lady Nancy, 41
Auden, W.H., 30
Augustine, St., 164
Aurelius, Marcus, 41

Bacall, Lauren, 116
Bachardy, Don, 12-13
Bacon, Sir Francis, 45
Bacon, Anthony, 45, 110
Bacon, Kevin, 141
Baez, Joan, 8, 116
Baker, Josephine, 41
Baldwin, James, 30, 66
Ball, Lucille, 116
Bang, Herman, 143
Bankhead, Tallulah, 8, 87
Banned, books with gay themes, 148-151, 153-154, 155
Banton, Buju, 117
Barber, Samuel, 11, 32
Barbette, 180
Barney, Natalie, 120, 177
Barresi, Paul, 27
Barrett, Rona, 116
Barrymore, Lionel, 139
Bashings, prominent gay, 128-129
Bates, Alan, 19
Bauman, Robert, 110, 114
Beard, James, 32
Beardsley, Aubrey, 90-91
Beaton, Cecil, 84
Beatty, Warren, 94
Beauvoir, Simone de, 116
Benedict IX (Pope), 165
Bennett, Michael, 170
Benny, Jack, 139
Bentham, Jeremy, 115
Berger, Helmut, 140
Berle, Milton, 87
Bernhard, Sandra, 23
Bernstein, Leonard, 30, 191
Bernstorff, Count Albrecht von, 175-176
Bestsellers, gay, 144-145
Bible, supposed references to homosexuality in, 34-35
Blake, Amanda, 169
Bobbitt, John Wayne, 92-93
Bogosian, Eric, 9
Bolger, Ray, 139
Bonin, William G., 106
Boswell, John, 35
Botticelli, Sandro, 110
Bowie, David, 9
Boy George, 6, 7, 27-28, 93
Boyd, Malcolm, 7
Boys, men who loved, 184-187
Boys in the Band, The, 63, 65, 129-130, 157
Brando, Marlon, 8, 93, 140
Bravo, Tony, 167
Bridges, Jeff, 140
Britten, Benjamin, 11-12, 31, 198
Broderick, Matthew, 19
Brooks, Garth, 116
Brooks, Louise, 8
Brothers, gay, 45-47
Brynner, Yul, 140
Buber, Martin, 115
Burnett, Carol, 116
Burr, Raymond, 7
Burroughs, William S., 7, 32, 187
Burton, Richard, 8
Burton, Sir Richard, 79, 84, 115
Businesses, provocatively named, 98
Button, Dick, 128-129
Byrnes, Edd, 139
Byron, Lord, 86

Cabaret, 157
Cadmus, Paul, 65
Caine, Michael, 19, 140
Califia, Pat, 150
Candy, John, 140
Capote, Truman, 30, 65, 118
Caravaggio, 89-90
Carlyle, Robert, 19
Carne, Judy, 8
Carpenter, Edward, 13, 196
Carson, Johnny, 93
Carswell, G. Harrold, 110, 113
Carter, Chip, 116
Cartland, Barbara, 119
Casanova, Giovanni Giacomo, 8, 79
Catullus, 184
Causes, alleged of homosexuality, 39, 48-51
Cavafy, Constantine, 46-47, 187
Censorship, 148-159
Chambers, Whittaker, 8
Chaney, Lon, 139
Chaplin, Charles, 87, 139
Characteristics, alleged of gays, 42, 55
Charles II, 87
Cheever, John, 32
Children's Hour, The, 154-155
Christianity, 13, 34-40, 54, 162-165
Christians, early homophobic, 162-165
Churchill, Winston, 8
Circumcised, men, 94
City and the Pillar, The, 155
Claiborne, Craig, 31
Clarke, Arthur C., 8
Clay, Andrew Dice, 64
Clement of Alexandria, 163
Clift, Montgomery, 110, 113
Cobain, Kurt, 116
Cobb, Lee J., 140
Coco, James, 7
Cocteau, Jean, 147-148, 176-177, 178, 180
Cohn, Roy, 84, 118, 169
Coleman, Dabney, 141
Connors, Dave, 33, 167
Conradin of Sicily, 198
Cook, Captain James, 79
Cooper, Gary, 87
Corlan, Anthony, 19
Corll, Dean Allen, 103-104
Cornbury, Lord, 179
Costello, Lou, 139
Counterfeiters, The, 18
Countries, foreign, gays in military in, 33; homosexual acts decriminalized in, 108-109; homosexual acts still criminalized in, 109; same-sex marriages recognized in, 20
Cousteau, Jacques, 4
Cowell, Henry, 110
Crane, Stephen, 142
Crawford, Cindy, 26
Crisp, Quentin, 7
Croce-Spinelli, 197
Crosby, Bing, 139
Crowe, Russell, 19
Cruise, Tom, 24, 68, 94
Cruising, 133-134
Cukor, George, 32, 84, 195